Preaching Christ
in a Pluralistic Age

SERMONS BY CARL E. BRAATEN

Lutheran University Press
Minneapolis, Minnesota

Preaching Christ in a Pluralistic Age

SERMONS BY CARL E. BRAATEN

Copyright 2011 Lutheran University Press, an imprint of 1517 Media. All rights reserved. Expect for brief quotations in articles or reviews, no part of this book may be reproduced in any manner without written permission of the publisher: 1517 Media Permissions, PO Box 1209, Minneapolis, MN 55440-1209, or copyright@1517.media.

Sculpture on cover is by A. Malcolm Gimse.

Library of Congress Cataloging-in-Publication Data

Braaten, Carl E., 1929-
    Preaching Christ in a pluralistic age : sermons / by Carl E. Braaten.
       p. cm.
    ISBN-13: 978-1-932688-62-7 (alk. paper)
    ISBN-10: 1-932688-62-5 (alk. paper)
    eISBN: 978-1-942304-73-9
    1. Lutheran Church—Sermons. 2. Sermons, American—21st century. I. Title.
    BX8066.B65P74 2011
    252'.041--dc23
                             2011020324

To

MY CHILDREN
Craig, Martha, Maria, Kristofer

MY GRANDCHILDREN
Jennifer, James, Sylvia, Linnea, Jake, Dana
Sean, Sonja, Ransom, Lennon, Bergen

MY GREAT-GRANDCHILDREN
Jonathon, Carson, Rylee, Carly

Contents

Preface 7

Part One: God and Christ 11
1. The Quest for Truth and the Trinity 13
2. The Humility and Humiliation of God 18
3. The Mystery and the Message 24
4. Who Is Jesus Christ for Us Today? 29
5. John and Jesus: A Study in Contrasts 34
6. Christ Is the Mystery of the World 39

Part Two: The Spirit and the Church 45
7. The House of God 47
8. After Easter, the Church! 54
9. Rekindling the Flame 58

Part Three: Evangelism and Mission 67
10. Evangelism: The Heart of the Church's Mission 69
11. No Other Gospel! 78
12. The Gospel and Religious Pluralism 83
13. God Made Manifest 89
14. The Coming of God in Human Flesh 94

Part Four: Reformation and Ecumenism 99
15. Shadows of the Cross 101
16. By Grace Through Faith in Christ 108

17. The Happy Exchange 114
18. The Vertical and Horizontal Dimensions of Forgiveness 120
19. The Reformation in an Ecumenical Age 125

Part Five: Ministry and Sacraments 133
20. Engaged in the Ministry 135
21. Believing and Behaving as Disciples 141
22. Love Never Ends 146
23. O Death, Where Is Your Victory? 149

Part Six: Death and Resurrection 153
24. God Put Death to Death in Raising Jesus 155
25. Lazarus and Jesus: Thoughts on Death and Resurrection 162
26. The Last Things 168

Preface

When I entered Luther Seminary in St. Paul, Minnesota, to study for the ordained ministry, my expectation was that I would become a pastor. And that I did, but only for three years. Then I became a professor of systematic theology at the Lutheran School of Theology at Chicago. I did that for thirty years. Although I was no longer preparing a sermon to deliver every Sunday morning, I continued to preach whenever I was invited to do so. That happened mostly in seminary chapels, in congregations of which my family and I were members, at family weddings, baptisms, confirmations, funerals, and on festival occasions in various churches throughout the land.

My first book of sermons is entitled *The Whole Counsel of God*, published by Fortress Press, 1974. I never claimed to be able to preach or even understand the entire mystery of God revealed in Christ, but I believe that should be our aim as ministers of the Word. My second book of sermons is entitled *Stewards of the Mysteries: Sermons for Festivals and Special Occasions*, published by Augsburg Publishing House, 1983. A steward is a person who acts as an agent of another. The Apostle Paul wrote, "For we do not proclaim ourselves; we proclaim Jesus Christ as Lord and ourselves as slaves for Jesus' sake" (2 Corinthians 4:5). I have entitled this third book of sermons *Preaching Christ in a Pluralistic Age*.

We live in an age of radical pluralism. One might ask, what's new about that? The earliest generation of Christians found themselves in a pluralistic situation from the beginning. They were witnessing to Jews as well as to Greeks and Romans in the great melting pot of Hellenistic culture. Moreover, the very concept of the church as the *ecclesia* of God meant that its members were called into being from many nations, each with its own religion and culture. The church's message of redemption is tailor-made for the manifold world of God's creation with all its wonderful variety of social and cultural forms. The church has never been monolithic. Pluralism is a positive dimension of the life of the one, holy, catholic, and apostolic church. Church history gives ample evidence of a plurality of creedal and doctrinal expressions as well as of liturgical, devotional, and artistic expressions.

We should be clear: Pluralism as such is not the enemy of the gospel. We take for granted that preaching the Christian message will always encounter a world with many religions, world views, ideologies, and lifestyles. Religious diversity is simply a fact. However, religious pluralism does pose a threat when it becomes an ideological dogma that asserts that all religions are equally valid and lead to the same goal. Such an ideology breeds the spirit of relativism, leading to the proverbial twilight in which "all cats are gray." Supposedly, no religion can be tolerated as more true or superior to others. It is all a matter of choice, of personal taste or preference. Many of the sermons in this volume challenge the pluralistic theology of religion that effectively nullifies the Great Commission to preach the gospel to all the nations.

From a human point of view there is no denying that the Christian faith is one option among many. As preachers we realize that the age of Christendom is over; Christianity no longer exists as the only sanctioned religion in the West. The Christian voice is now only one among many. No, that is not quite right. There are many voices that claim to be Christian, and some contradict each other. In the early church, the gnostics gave the apostolic faith of the New Testament a run for its money. The author of the *Letter of Jude* found it necessary to appeal to his fellow believers "to contend for the faith that was once for all entrusted to the saints" (Jude 3). This is no less necessary today. But no preacher can do it alone. We have the resources of a great tradition to help us tell the difference between preaching Christ and preaching ourselves. Gnosticism is the perennial religion that locates the great mystery of the world within the self. It is the task of doctrinal preaching to separate the wheat from the chaff, true from false interpretations of the biblical message.

Our aim in preaching is to be faithful to the revelation of the triune God in Holy Scripture. Faithfulness is not decided by the individual preacher's say-so; rather, the community of believers will judge whether these sermons—or any others—conform to the truths confessed in the ancient creeds and confessions. The creeds identify not only what Christians explicitly affirm, but also what they implicitly deny. Most of the creedal statements were formulated to refute false teachings that contested the truth of the gospel. The sermons in this volume are mostly didactic; they teach the faith as I understand it. They are doctrinal; they assert and defend the truths of the classical Christian tradition and in the process identify false teachings that threaten the integrity of the gospel. I agree with what Luther said to Erasmus: "Nothing is better known or more common among Christians than assertion. Take away assertions and you take away Christianity" (Martin Luther, *The Bondage of the Will, Luther's Works*, Vol. 33. Fortress Press. p. 21).

H. Richard Niebuhr once characterized Protestant preaching as a "unitarianism of the second article." I plead guilty in a sense, because I am convinced that even a robust doctrine of the Trinity is dependent on what we believe about Jesus. We know who the Father is because we first came to know his Son. As for the Spirit, the third person of the Trinity, he is the Spirit sent by the Son. Apart from Jesus Christ we do not know the Father or the Spirit.

Since these sermons are unabashedly Christocentric in the order of our knowledge of God, it is not surprising that they enter into the most controversial issues of Christology today. Is Jesus really the one the evangelists claimed him to be? Jesus is the Messiah, but is he truly God? Can moderns still believe that God became human in a real incarnation? Was the resurrection of Jesus a historical event; that is, did Jesus rise bodily from the dead? Is Jesus the sole Savior of humankind? Have Catholics and Lutherans reached an ecumenical consensus on the doctrine of justification by faith? Should churches today be engaged in a mission to evangelize all the nations, no matter what their culture or religion? What is the nature of the Christian hope for life beyond death? These are some of the questions taken up in these sermonic essays.

I believe that if Christianity is not true, it is not worth the bother. In his book, *After Virtue*, Alasdair MacIntyre writes that the value of reasoned argument has simply disappeared. Even in the academy there is a presumption in favor of feeling over thought. What is taken as decisive is how people feel about themselves, how they feel about things, about the tradition, about others. When asked to comment on a text, students frequently begin their response by saying, "I feel that . . ." instead of saying, "I think that. . . ." As an academic theologian I prize thinking over feeling whenever the matter of truth is at stake. I do not depreciate the importance of emotion in religion, but in itself that cannot answer the question whether to be a Christian, what to believe, and how to behave.

Polls indicate that the Christian faith is losing its grip on the western European and American mind. Churches are engaged in high-level studies on how to meet the challenge of secularism. Some endorse the strategy of accommodating contemporary culture, saying *"gesundheit"* whenever the world sneezes. The notion is widespread that, to attract people to our churches, we had better make sure that our product is what consumers want and is that for which they are willing to pay. Certain techniques to make congregations grow and become successful in terms of members, budgets, buildings, and programs might work in the short run. But in the long run the only thing that will sustain the church through thick and thin is what kept the martyrs faithful during times of persecution—firm confidence in the biblical truth that God revealed himself in the life, death, and resurrection of Jesus. This revelation promises eternal salvation to all who believe.

It is worrisome that the theological IQ of the mainline churches has been declining to the point that much of contemporary preaching has become weak and vacuous, subjective and sentimental, incapable of taking Christian doctrine seriously. The result is that a subtle shift has taken place from a theocentric to an anthropocentric perspective. The trends and fads of the day usurp the place once given to the biblical narratives and church traditions to which they gave rise. A paradigm shift has occurred from preaching the sturdy doctrines that explain the truths of the faith to the telling of stories that make people giggle and feel good.

My hope is that these sermons will support the belief that true Christian worship includes a special time for celebrating the presence of God through audible words of preaching and the visible words of Holy Communion. This should make clear that the church is utterly different from the world, by stressing that the gospel it proclaims is unique to Christianity and different from other religions and ideologies. What the church has to offer the world cannot be provided by any other agency or organization. We believe there is salvation in no other name than the holy name of Jesus the Christ. And because the church is the body of Christ, there is in that sense no salvation outside the church. That does not accord with the popular pluralistic theory of religions, but that is what the New Testament says. That is where we wish to take our stand as Luther did in his day, no matter how much that might offend what is deemed to be politically correct.

Lent, 2011

PART ONE

God and Christ

> In Christ God was reconciling the world to himself.
> (2 Corinthians 5:19b)

This one brief statement contains the truth of the gospel. The sermons in Part One are foundational for everything that we believe, preach, and teach concerning the Christian faith. They speak of the triune God and of his Son Jesus Christ. In contrast, a lot of talk about God goes on without making clear which of the many gods in the pantheon of the world's religions is being discussed.

Adolf von Harnack, chief architect of modern Protestant theology, wrote in *What Is Christianity?*: "The gospel that Jesus preached has to do only with the Father, and not with the Son. . . . It is perverse to make Christology the fundamental substance of the gospel" (pp. 144, 184).

A Christ-centered theology is both trinitarian and monotheistic. The answer to how it can be both is enshrined in the mystery of the gospel these sermons try to explicate as clearly as possible.

1

The Quest for Truth and the Trinity

John 16:13-15:

> When the Spirit of truth comes, he will guide you into all the truth; for he will not speak on his own, but will speak whatever he hears, and he will declare to you the things that are to come. He will glorify me, because he will take what is mine and declare it to you. All that the Father has is mine. For this reason I said that he will take what is mine and declare it to you.

The Search for Truth

I believe that God created human beings with a profound desire to learn new things. There is no limit to what we want to know. As wanderers in the wilderness of ignorance, we long to discover one day the promised land of truth. Our life is a voyage bent on discovering things never known before.

So it was with Christopher Columbus. The old ditty tells us that Columbus sailed the ocean blue, and discovered America in 1492. That is the way we learned it; we thought it was absolutely true. Now our children tell us that is not the way it was. Someone made a poster that reads: "Indians Discovered America." Columbus had no inkling of what he was actually doing. He was in search of a shorter route to Asia when he landed on an island, and ever since that time the islands off our southeastern coast are misleadingly called the West Indies. Columbus died believing that he had found only a new way to the old world.

The spirit of discovery cannot be quenched. There is a bit of Christopher Columbus in each one of us. Perhaps that is in part what we mean by saying that we are created in "the image of God." We have a built-in urge to learn the truth, to discover something new—*terra incognita*. As humans we are finite, confined within the boundaries of space and time. Yet we are driven by a deep impulse to strive for what lies beyond. We are never satisfied to live within the limits of the existence we now know. We seem to be always striving to exceed the boundaries, to explore new frontiers, and to discover new worlds.

The eighteenth century German philosopher, Gotthold Ephraim Lessing, put it quite well. If God were holding all the truth in the world in his right hand, and in his left hand he held the restless urge to find the truth, then came to you and said, "Choose," which would you choose? Lessing said, "I would humbly fall upon God's left hand and say, 'Father, give me this. Pure truth is surely for thee alone!' " Lessing put his finger on that part of the human spirit that refuses to have its wings clipped and its feet tethered. This is what St. Augustine meant when he said, "The human heart is restless until it finds its rest in thee, O Lord."

Despite what atheists think, a deep search for ultimate truth—for God—pulsates in the human heart. In the book of Job, Zophar the Naamathite poses this question: "Can you find out the deep things of God? Can you find out the limit of the Almighty? It is higher than heaven—what can you do? Deeper than Sheol—what can you know?" (Job 11:7-8).

People in all cultures and religions are searching for truth, but they do not necessarily call it "God." When I was at Harvard University, I was impressed with the sign *"Veritas"*—the Latin word for "truth"—inscribed on its bulletins and buildings. That was the educational ideal of the Puritan founders of the university. Yet according to opinion polls, the majority of today's students and professors seeking after truth do not profess belief in God. Most are at best agnostic, not sure whether or not there is a God.

Still, if people are searching for ultimate truth with deep passion and love, they are in some way seeking after "God," even though they do not know God's name. As Christians we confess that Christ is the truth. This does not mean we devalue the quest for truth wherever it takes place. We believe that whenever people find a bit of truth, they are at least touching the edge of God's truth.

We believe the Holy Spirit is leading people into all the truth there is, whether the small truths of physics and chemistry, the bigger truths of history and philosophy, or the still larger truths of religion and revelation. For all truth is of God, and the Spirit is at work inwardly to motivate and guide the universal human quest for truth.

The Arrival of Truth

We have this promise that when the Spirit of truth comes, he will guide us into all truth. All truth? All the truth there is to know of biology? All there is to learn about astronomy? Everything about history and psychology and medicine and computers? Like many people in our privileged culture, I have spent a major part of my life going to school, yet I do not claim to know more than a minor portion of all truth. Being a Christian has not provided any shortcuts. The newspapers continue to report court battles over evolution and creation science. Groups of fundamentalist Christians are trying to enact into law the teaching of the Bible as a textbook on science that provides direct scientific knowledge on how the world began.

Christians are mistaken when they read the Bible as a book on creation science, giving us all the truth about how the world began. That is not what the Spirit of truth is doing in the world. "He will take what is mine," Jesus says, "and declare it to you" (John 16:13b). That is not a substitute for the many truths of science and philosophy, nor is it a shortcut to knowledge that we can learn only by research and reason. As the way to the truth of life eternal, the Spirit is at work to guide us into all the truth that counts, the decisive truth about our life and its final meaning and goal.

How do we come to know the truth of Christ? It happens as a miracle, not as a reward for hard work. It comes as a gift, perhaps when you least expect it. The truth is a Person who comes to meet you and take you by surprise.

A little farm boy in South Africa found a shiny pebble and played with it as a toy. It turned out to be a diamond that led to further discovery of diamond fields. Just a pebble, it contained the promise of vast treasures. Columbus set out to find Old China; what he found was a new world.

We too have set some goals and have worked hard to meet them. Perhaps it was to get a college degree, land a good job, gain a promotion, run for office, win a prize, finish a book, or any one of a thousand things, but the joy of achieving does not last. The glamour of the moment vanishes, and history does not long remember our great deeds.

Here is the great secret of Christian experience. While we are on the way—earnestly pursuing our goals, believing that when we attain them we will be happy and feel fulfilled—we are stopped in our tracks by meeting someone—perhaps a Christian witness—who reveals to us "the pearl of great price," the ultimate meaning of truth, an absolute goal that goes infinitely beyond all our rather measly aims in life. We learn that the truth of life is not in what we discover, but in being discovered, not in what we achieve, but in what God has already done for us. We may spend a lifetime looking for God, until that day when we wake up to the great truth that he has already found us. "For while we were still weak, at the right time Christ died for the ungodly" (Romans 5:6).

The Name of Truth

What do we really know about truth? There is the truth of a proposition. Two plus two equals four. Two parts of hydrogen to one part of oxygen makes water. That is also a true proposition. But there is a deeper kind of truth, one that comes to light in personal encounter. Jesus said, "I am the way, and the truth, and the life. No one comes to the Father except through me" (John 14:6). That is truth that lies in a name.

You never know a person, not really, until you know the person's name. There's magic in a name. When you are introduced to a stranger, the first exchange of words is to learn each other's names.

In our restless search for God, we never really come to know him until we learn his name. We want to know him on a first name basis. This is what Martin Buber called an "I-Thou relationship." Many religions hold an impersonal idea of God. Many people searching for "God" have no clear concept of who or what he is. In the words of John Updike, God for them is an "oblong blur."

The Bible pictures God as one who personally speaks and reveals himself. In the Old Testament, God spoke to Moses and told him his name is "Jahweh," which means "I am who I am." In the New Testament, Jesus gave us a personal name for God as "Abba," which means "Daddy" or "Papa." As followers of Jesus we also call God "Our Father" in the prayer he taught us to pray.

Because of the intimate relationship between Jesus and the Father, we have an expanded list of names of God. Jesus is the "Son of God," because he reveals the true nature of the one whom he called his "Father." Like Father, like Son! Thus, the Father is God, and the Son is God, and so is the Holy Spirit who proceeds from the Father through the Son. The one God has three personal names—Father, Son, and Holy Spirit.

The struggle continues in the church to understand the nature of the divine truth that has arrived in Jesus Christ. The classic conflict between a unitarian and a trinitarian interpretation of truth is still going on in modern theology. There are still theologians who think: If God is one, he cannot be three! Some call the Trinity—the idea that the one God is at the same time three persons—a mystery, a paradox, even a dialectical statement; others call it absurd, a contradiction, even nonsensical.

With the chorus of confessors in the one, holy, catholic church, we believe and teach the truth that God is one, and that this one God is Father, Son, and Holy Spirit. It is a mystery, to be sure; it cannot be grasped fully by reason. But only as Triune can we most adequately speak of the true God who has arrived in Jesus Christ for our salvation and the world's. This knowledge of the Trinity is bound to our confession of Jesus as our Lord and Savior. The Spirit of truth glorifies the Father in the Son. Here we have the heartbeat of the Christian faith and the mighty meaning of the gospel. Amen.

2

The Humility and Humiliation of God

Philippians 2:5-11:
> Let the same mind be in you that was in Christ Jesus,
> who, though he was in the form of God,
> did not regard equality with God
> as something to be exploited,
> but emptied himself, taking the form of a slave,
> being born in human likeness.
> And being found in human form,
> he humbled himself
> and became obedient to the point of death—
> even death on a cross.
> Therefore God also highly exalted him
> and gave him the name
> that is above every name,
> so that at the name of Jesus
> every knee should bend,
> in heaven and on earth and
> under the earth,
> and every tongue should confess
> that Jesus Christ is Lord,
> to the glory of God the Father.

Today there is a growing interest in the religions of the world, partly because of their political impact on current events. Moreover, as complex systems of belief, the religions are no longer practiced merely in distant lands. They have found their way to our shores. As we encounter persons of other religions, we are challenged to discover what they believe, teach, and practice. The child sitting next to you in school may be a Hindu. The woman at the checkout counter may be a Buddhist. One of the NBA superstars may be a Muslim. We are curious to learn the distinctive characteristics of each of these religions, especially in comparison to Christianity.

Once I was commissioned to serve on a task force to draft a statement concerning the Lutheran response to the challenge of today's plurality of religions. We were reminded that the essence of the Muslim religion is submission to the will of Allah. Submission is the meaning of the word "Islam." The essence of Hinduism is unification, becoming one with Brahman, the supreme source of life. The core belief of Buddhism is enlightenment; it's believed to be the solution to the problem of suffering.

What is the essence of Christianity? Can we define it in a single word or sentence? As members of the task force, we sat around our study table, comparing Christianity with other religions. We tried a thought experiment. If we had to choose just one word to define Christianity, what would it be? High on our list were words like incarnation, reconciliation, forgiveness, justification, atonement, or resurrection.

Or, if we had to choose just one sentence, what would it be? If you were the first missionary to Borneo, witnessing to people who had never heard one word of the gospel, what would you tell them? You could hardly do better than John 3:16: "For God so loved the world that he gave his only Son, so that everyone who believes in him may not perish but may have eternal life." Another favorite is from the pen of the Apostle Paul: "In Christ God was reconciling the world to himself" (2 Corinthians 5:19). How about the prologue of the Gospel of John? There it says: "In the beginning was the Word, and the Word was with God, and the Word was God. . . . And the Word became flesh and lived among us" (John 1:1; 1:14). The gospel goes on to tell the story of Jesus' life and ministry. Martin Luther found the greatest life-saving truth in Romans and Galatians. They teach that "a person is justified by faith in Christ alone apart from works of the law." There are so many similar one-liners of equal power in the Bible.

The Humility of God

The verse that I have chosen to dwell on in particular is contained in Paul's letter to the Philippians: "Let the same mind be in you that was in Christ Jesus, who, though he was in the form of God, did not regard equality with God as something to be exploited, but emptied himself, taking the form of a slave, being born in human likeness. And being found in human form, he humbled himself and became obedient to the point of death—even death on a cross."

Here we have the classic statement of what Christian theology calls the doctrine of *kenosis*. The word *kenosis* in Greek means emptying. Christ Jesus emptied himself of his divine attributes of omnipotence and omniscience, eternal glory and honor, kingly power and privilege. In so emptying himself, he humbled himself to become a human being. Jesus of Nazareth was born in a barn. He grew up as a Jewish boy in the one-horse town of Nazareth. He walked the streets with lepers and kept company with sinners.

The eternal Son of God, equal with the Father in heaven, is the rabbi who rode into Jerusalem on a colt. He did not come riding on a big white steed like a conquering general. The king of the universe came riding on a donkey—a symbol of humility. This man is God *incognito*. He really is God, though he does not look like it, because he has divested himself of his omni-attributes. He could have remained in his heavenly abode. He could have retained all the rights and privileges of the royal throne. He set all of that aside to enter the life of a lowly human being. Why would he do that? Why did he give up the cozy comforts of his heavenly home to take on the struggles of life that we all know about? Why did God become a human being?

Søren Kierkegaard, a Danish Lutheran philosopher in the nineteenth century, asked the question, "What made God do it? Why did the infinite God become a finite human being?" Kierkegaard tells the parable about a king who loved a lowly maiden. The king had a problem: How should he woo her? How should he win her love for no other reason than from the purest motive of love? If he presented himself as a king to the humble maiden, their inequality would be overwhelming. She might be overly impressed by his pomp and power. She might be moved to honor him as her superior. She might be attracted to him for the wrong reasons.

True love should have the power to erase inequality, so that the two become one. But a king and a maiden? Hardly. The king decided that the union would have to be brought about in some other way. He would have to descend from his lofty status as king and become her equal in the form of a servant. He would have to humble himself and appear as one willing to serve. This would have to be real, not a mere charade.

That is a parable of what God did. The King of kings became a humble servant, on account of his love. He came down to our level to become our equal. He would have to be willing to suffer as we do and experience all the typical things that fall to our lot.

The Humiliation of Jesus

Palm Sunday is the beginning of the week that transforms the humility of God into the greatest humiliation the world has ever known, the suffering and dying of God the Son on the cross. Moving from the state of humility to humiliation, he was willing to suffer hunger in the desert, thirst at the time of his agony, and forsakenness in the hour of his dying—so great was God's love for us. "In this is love, not that we loved God but that he loved us and sent his Son to be the atoning sacrifice for our sins" (1 John 4:10).

On Palm Sunday the multitude of Jesus' friends and followers arranged a great parade. They were ecstatic. Filled with joy, they shouted, "Hosanna! Blessed is the one who comes in the name of the Lord" (Mark 11:9b). It was great street theater. Everyone had a good time, singing and dancing in the streets. But they had no idea what was coming next—Jesus walking into the jaws of death. On the way, he would suffer betrayal by the kiss of Judas, denial by Peter, and desertion by all his disciples. He stumbled and fell as he dragged the old rugged cross up the hill. He was spit on, slapped, and beaten; he was nailed to the cross between two criminals.

This was not merely a case of justice run amok, a violation of the rights of an innocent man. This was the humiliation of the Son of God. He suffered and died, but it did not end there. He was buried in a borrowed grave. Then, as the Apostles' Creed says, "He descended into hell." Lower than that one cannot get. He came down from heaven and ended up in Hades.

We love to hear stories of "rags to riches," but this is the other way around, from the glorious company of heaven to the wretched of the earth, and finally all the way down to the bottom of the pit, the place called "hell." Don't ask me to explain that! I have never been there and cannot tell you anything about it except—believe me—it is not the kind of journey any of us would want to plan for our future.

Have This Mind in You

We have been exploring the meaning of two words that apply to the story of Christ Jesus: humility and humiliation. The incarnation of God in a human life expresses the humility of God. His death on the cross shows forth the humiliation of God. What does this mean for us who have neither given up the glory of heaven nor endured the indignities of Passion Week as Jesus did? There is meaning in it for us; otherwise Paul would not have said, "Let the same mind be in you that was in Christ Jesus."

The eternal Lord was willing to give up his lofty status to become a lowly servant on account of his love. In giving up equality with God, he chose to become equal with us, so that we might become equal with him. Because he attached himself to our flesh and blood, every human being has received a new identity and a new dignity. All persons, without exception, have become infinitely precious and valuable in God's sight, because Christ came to earth to lift us up, to exalt those of low estate.

Once I was summoned for jury duty to the Maricopa County Courthouse in downtown Phoenix. As I walked from the parking lot, I saw as many as five homeless people sleeping among the hedges by the sidewalk—crumpled little bodies they were, barely visible under a bunch of rags. I had a sinking feeling. I asked myself, how should I look upon these poor wretched folks? They were not asking for anything. But still I had a problem—my attitude to them! What was in my mind? Am I superior? Should I thank God that I am not one of them? On further thought I asked, if I took on the mind of Christ, what then would I think? The answer dawned on me that no matter what the predicament of these homeless people, they are all human beings created in the image of God, just a little lower than the angels. They bear the imprint of God upon their heart, mind, and soul. So in that respect there is no distinction among us. Secondly, they are all individuals for whom Christ died and for whom he was raised from the tomb. That means they are loved by God infinitely and absolutely. For us to recognize that is to share the mind of Christ.

There is a sequel to the story of Christ's humiliation. In Holy Week we travel with Christ along the *via dolorosa,* the way of suffering, observing the stations of the cross. But after his humiliating treatment to the point of death, a great reversal took place. He passed from humiliation to the state of exaltation. As our text says, "Therefore God also highly exalted him and gave him the name that is above every name, so that at the name of Jesus every knee should bend, in heaven and on earth and under the earth, and every tongue should confess that Jesus Christ is Lord, to the glory of God the Father" (Philippians 2:9-11).

We began this sermon talking about world religions. After his resurrection Jesus commissioned his disciples to preach the gospel in his name to all the nations. Those early Christians were not wise by human standards. They were not strong and powerful; they were not born of nobility. But they went forth in the strong name of Jesus, the super name which is above all other names. On account of the missionary movement, beginning with the apostles, believers in Christ have crisscrossed the world, exalting him among the nations. And at last the kingdoms of this world will become the kingdom of our God and Lord, and he shall reign forever and ever. Amen.

3

The Mystery and the Message

Ephesians 3:2-12:

> For surely you have already heard of the commission of God's grace that was given me for you, and how the mystery was made known to me by revelation. . . . In former generations this mystery was not made known to humankind, as it has now been revealed to his holy apostles and prophets by the Spirit: that is, the Gentiles have become fellow heirs, members of the same body, and sharers in the promise in Christ Jesus through the gospel. Of this gospel I have become a servant according to the gift of God's grace that was given me by the working of his power. Although I am the very least of all the saints, this grace was given to me to bring to the Gentiles the news of the boundless riches of Christ, and to make everyone see what is the plan of the mystery hidden for ages in God who created all things; so that through the church the wisdom of God in its rich variety might now be made known to the rulers and authorities in the heavenly places. This was in accordance with the eternal purpose that he has carried out in Christ Jesus our Lord, in whom we have access to God in boldness and confidence through faith in him.

The Mystery of the Gospel

We have read one of the most magnificent passages in the whole of Scripture. The apostle Paul here sets forth his apostolic theology in a nutshell: Christ is the deep mystery of the universe, a mystery that has been revealed to the holy apostles by the Spirit of God. Paul—who not many years earlier was out to kill the followers of Jesus—was now a minister of the great mystery, a minister with a message on a mission to reach the Gentiles.

My aim in this sermon is to teach the meaning of this great mystery—the mystery of Christ at the heart of the universe. We are living in a time of great ambiguity. On the one hand, ours is a secular age that wants to know nothing about mystery and miracle. It limits knowledge to the five senses—what we can see, hear, taste, touch, and smell. On the other hand, ours is a very religious age, with people searching for new and exotic forms of spirituality. Today's bookstores are bulging with bestsellers touting arcane cults, black magic, Satanism, and secret societies. People are bored by the one-dimensional thinking of the secularist view of the world.

The modern church is in danger of losing the sense of the mystery of the gospel. Many church leaders and theologians want to boil down the Christian faith to what is supposedly relevant or reasonable. All sorts of trends threaten to take the mystery out of the faith and to make the gospel serve their own purposes. Some do it with psychology, to make people feel good. Some do it with politics, to promote the ideology of their choice.

Taking the mystery out of the faith is like taking oil out of the lamp. The result is that there is no fire, no heat, no light. The mystery of Christ at the heart of the universe is the secret power of our faith. It is the one great truth. There are many lesser truths, of course, and we can learn them from history, literature, philosophy, and the sciences. That's what we go to school for so many years to learn. We may even top it off with a Ph.D.

The one great mystery of Christ is not something one can learn in school. It comes only through the church, through its preaching of the gospel, and it is received through faith alone. We cannot believe in it by our unaided reason. We can learn many wonderful things from the great books, the classics of antiquity, but the one thing we really need to know of absolute worth comes from only one source, namely, the Bible, the Word of God, the sacred book of the church—not from Plato, Shakespeare, Kant, or Einstein.

We can never fully plumb the depths of the mystery of Christ revealed to us in the Bible and through the church. After a lifetime of studious analysis, the mystery remains no less a mystery. In theology we try to formulate certain gospel axioms to keep our thinking straight about it. Orthodoxy means "straight thinking." Heresy means "crooked thinking." The greatest heresy is to confuse the one great mystery of our faith with some lesser truths, from philosophy, religion, or ideology. Certain fundamental axioms—seven in all—can help to keep our thinking straight about the mystery of Christ and the message of the gospel that is our mission to bring to all the nations.

Seven Gospel Axioms

1. The first one is contained in the two words our Lord taught us to pray: "Our Father." We belong to God; we are created by God; we are not our own. We do not even own our bodies, to do with as we please. We are children of our heavenly Father, rooted and grounded in the being of God who created heaven and earth.

2. The God who made us loves us and accepts us for Jesus' sake. This love is a pure gift; it is absolutely free; and it spells salvation, liberation from sin, death, and the power of Satan.

   The great theologian, Karl Barth, once was asked—after he had written many tomes of church dogmatics—to sum up the whole Christian faith in a few words. He answered, "Jesus loves me, this I know, for the Bible tells me so."

3. The old story of Jesus and his love is equally valid and true for all people, of whatever color, culture, religion, class, age, or gender. Some people today say that all religions are equal, equally true and valid as ways of salvation. But that is not what Paul says. The mystery of God was hidden for ages, but now in these latter days it has been revealed, so that all the Gentiles too might believe and share the new life in Christ.

4. Never think that this message is a product of human imagination. If we created it, we would own it; we could put our own logo or label on it. But that is not the way it is. It is solely a matter of God's revelation; flesh and blood did not reveal it unto us. It is not Lutheran, nor Protestant, nor Roman, nor Greek. It came down to us from heaven; it is the Word of God. It is not the result of scientific research, artistic creativity, or transcendental meditation.

5. This axiom is equally important: the gospel message is the power of God unto salvation. The Greek word for power is *dynamis*—dynamite. Yet the gospel seems so weak. It shares the weakness of the crucified Jesus who hung on a cross, while people scoffed at him, saying: "If you are the King of the Jews, save yourself" (Luke 23:37). This is a great mystery, how the cross of Christ can be the power of God to save a world that respects mainly the threat of armies, tanks, and nuclear war-heads. The temptation of the church is to hanker after the worldly kind of power, to

flex its political muscle, and to seek big headlines that magnify its public image. Some of the so-called mega-churches advertise their remarkable growth in worldly ways, measured in terms of membership, budgets, and buildings! But according to the gospel, we live and die by the sign of the cross, the power of God unto salvation for all who believe in Jesus.

6. The Christian life begins and ends with doxology, the praise of God from whom all blessings flow. The first question that appears in the Westminster Catechism is: "Why did God create man?" The answer is: "To glorify God and to enjoy him forever." God is the sole end and purpose of human existence, because God is the absolute source of all that is true, good, and beautiful. This is why worship in "fear and trembling" is the most proper way to approach the mystery of God at the heart of the universe.

7. Seven is a sacred number in the Bible, so it is fitting to offer a seventh gospel axiom to keep our thinking straight. What we share in Christ is the hope of eternal life. This life in the "here and now" is not all there is to it.

One evening my wife and I were listening to Larry King on his CNN talk show. He was interviewing three famous people—an architect, an author, and an actress. They had all done well and had acquired both fame and fortune. He had them reminiscing and reflecting on how they had reached the top in their respective fields, all starting from humble beginnings. They had done it by dint of hard work, perspiration, and a little bit of luck. Then he asked them, what about the future? "Do you believe in a life beyond this one?" And they all said "No." The life we experience "here and now" is all there is, with no hope for immortal life beyond the grave.

But the gospel says, death does not have the last word. Death has been put to death by the power of God in raising Jesus from the dead. Jesus is alive in the world today, and that means we are not alone. So we can meet our own death as people of promise and with hope, as people who look forward to a share of eternal life with God forever. Nothing can separate us from the love of God, not even death or the fear of death.

Faithful Witness to the Message

Those seven gospel axioms frame the holy mystery of God and the gospel of Jesus Christ. Many people seem to be worried about the church. They read the demographic trends of the mainline Protestant denominations. The predictions are pretty grim and hard to refute. Many churches are losing thousands of members; national budgets are shrinking; and the average age of church goers is getting higher.

I do not think we should worry much about such quantifiable things. What counts is that we remain as faithful witnesses to the mystery of Christ and the message of the first apostles. What difference does it make whether we grow smaller and older or younger and bigger, if we do not measure things qualitatively in terms of the gospel and the glory of God?

John F. Kennedy captured the imagination of the American people with his campaign slogan: "Let us get America moving again." It is time we say that about the church too. It is time to get going with the gospel. It is time to be on gospel alert for the mission God has given us, to preach the mystery of Christ to people in other religions and to people with no religion at all. We have a story to tell to the nations. We have a message that all persons need to hear, because we all need Christ. It is a message for the whole person, not only for the soul and lofty spiritual things, but for the body and down-to-earth physical things. This is a message of total salvation, for body, mind, and soul. Amen!

4

Who Is Jesus Christ for Us Today?

Matthew 16:13-17:

> Now when Jesus came into the district of Caesarea Philippi, he asked his disciples, "Who do people say that the Son of Man is?" And they said, "Some say John the Baptist, but others Elijah, and still others Jeremiah or one of the prophets." He said to them, "But who do you say that I am?" Simon Peter answered, "You are the Messiah, the Son of the living God." And Jesus answered him, "Blessed are you, Simon son of Jonah! For flesh and blood has not revealed this to you, but my Father in heaven."

The Modern Search for Jesus

The twentieth century is still grappling with the question Jesus addressed to his disciples at Caesarea Philippi: "Who do you say that I am?" It still strikes us with its original enigmatic force. Even many people who do not believe Jesus is the Messiah, the Son of the living God, have a high regard for his teachings and try to live according to them.

The story of the search for the so-called "Jesus of history" coincides with the beginning of modern Protestant theology. The land in which this search has bloomed, withered, and revived again and again is Germany. One of the truly exciting chapters in modern biblical scholarship has been the attempt to lay hold of the historical Jesus, as he really was, and then to figure out his true meaning for humanity and history. Since the eighteenth century, not only believers but scholars have been busy answering the question Jesus put at Caesarea Philippi: "Who do people say that I am?"

For over a millennium and a half the church had answered this question in the ancient creeds and councils of the church. We still recite the old formulae in the Apostles' Creed and the Nicene Creed, which build on Peter's confession. "We believe in one Lord Jesus Christ, the only Son of God, eternally begotten of the Father, God from God." These confessions affirm the true divinity and true humanity of Jesus Christ.

In the eighteenth century these creedal and confessional coverings were removed from the historical figure of Jesus. The old dogmas of the church were regarded as misleading and irrelevant. Scholars wanted to know the actual personality of the historical Jesus, the flesh-and-blood vitality of the real man, not merely what his followers believed and taught about him.

Biographers enjoy writing about the great figures of history. Artists and dramatists have been challenged to practice their skills on Jesus of Nazareth. Albert Schweitzer wrote what is now a classic: *The Quest of the Historical Jesus*. What he showed is that all the biographers failed. They all painted a portrait of Jesus as a fulfillment of their own wishes, as a projection of their own ideals. Behind the mass of scholarly details, we can see the image of each scholar superimposed on the picture of Jesus. Like plastic surgeons making over the face of the patient in their own image, or perhaps like artists who paint themselves into the figures they create, the modern biographical and psychological presentations have projected modern ideals and values upon the figure of Jesus they portray. They have all succumbed to what Professor Henry Cadbury of Harvard University called "The Peril of Modernizing Jesus."

If we look at the pictures of Jesus that appear in the albums of modern critical scholarship, we will see a bewildering variety. Jesus looks like an effete romanticist in Ernst Renan, a rationalistic deist in Heinrich Paulus, a God-intoxicated mystic in Friedrich Schleiermacher, a mythical hero in Bruno Bauer, an apocalyptic fanatic in Albert Schweitzer, or a socialist reformer among the Marxists. As we turn the pages we come to the contemporary section where we see a Jesus talking like an existentialist philosopher, or like the founder of the institute on positive mental attitude, or like a guerrilla fighter overthrowing the ruling class, or like the leader of the black power movement, etc. Jesus is treated as so much putty in the hands of clever people who use him to advance their own schemes and interests.

The Enigmatic Jesus

So how can we know for sure who Jesus really is? And what difference does it make, anyway? It may be that this weird collection of pictures of Jesus in the galleries of modern scholarship has something to say to us about the real nature of the person of Jesus. The very plurality of pictures may tell us that Jesus is not easy to understand. It may not be only our fault that, due to our stubborn wills and narrow minds, we cannot capture a credible image that we can all accept. This pluralism may point to the enigma of the person of Jesus, making it appear that he has many faces, depending on the angle from which one chooses to look. It may be that Jesus' extraordinary qualities account for the fact that he eludes our categories and transcends all our available analogies, even though he is truly a human being.

Jesus was a man, part of our history, sharing fully our kind of time and experience. He was very much like the rest of us. Yet, there is a great difference. The Nicene Creed says that he is so different, that only the biggest of all the little words in our vocabulary can fully capture the categorical difference: the word "God." He is truly human, but he is also "very God" and that puts him in a class of his own. So he is called the only-begotten Son, the one and only Savior, the one and only Lord, the one and only Messiah, the one and only Liberator. A long list of titles applies to Jesus, each bringing out a special aspect of his total being and meaning.

The New Testament contains virtually all the knowledge we possess concerning Jesus of Nazareth, the Christ, the Son of the living God, despite the Nag Hammadi discoveries of some Gnostic gospels. All of our knowledge concerning Jesus comes to us in the form of witness. No purely objective historical knowledge exists about this man, untouched by the impressions of faith and witness. Only believers in Christ have told us what it means to be followers of Jesus, so much so that they conflated the two terms, and simply called him "Jesus Christ," as though Christ were not a title, but the second name of Jesus.

If we should strip away all the titles, and then ask the real Jesus of history to stand up, nobody would respond. Nobody would answer to the name "Jesus," absent the titles of exaltation that distinguish his identity and memory in world history. There is no Jesus who is merely Jesus. Someone answering to the name "Jesus" might be playing baseball in one of the major leagues. When some radical scholars have stripped away all the titles of exaltation, they reached the irrational conclusion that Jesus of Nazareth never even existed. They discovered that it is like peeling an onion; there is no seed inside. They hypothesized that the story of Jesus was merely the creation of people who wanted to quit fishing, run a congregation, make an easy living, or something like that.

The Perspective of Faith

Now let us take a flying leap into the sixteenth century. Melanchthon, Luther's right hand man, said, "To know Christ is to know his benefits." That still stands as a wise statement on this side of modern critical scholarship. The New Testament abounds with titles that serve to identify the uniqueness of Jesus. We are not so sure what the historical Jesus thought about himself. He did not run around bragging about how great he is; he did not say he was Jesus Christ Superstar. He asked questions for which he did not give the answer, except the answer of his life and actions. Actions speak louder than words. So it was with Jesus. But the New Testament gives lots of answers. They are the answers of the followers of Jesus who believed he is the Christ.

There is a bias, to be sure, in the apostolic witness to Jesus, the Christ of the living God. It is the bias of faith. An apostolic bias of faith is at work in the earliest preaching and witness to Jesus. This bias is written into all the documents that give us any clue at all about Jesus. They talk about Jesus as the Christ, the Son of God, Lord, Savior, Logos, High Priest, Servant of God, Prophet, and many others. These titles were conferred upon Jesus in the light of their faith and experience of the appearance of the risen Jesus.

Some of the titles attribute to Jesus the functions of divinity. Jesus is called the Savior, but is it not true that only God can save? Jesus is the Lord, but is it not true that only God is the Lord of lords? Jesus is the Word, but is it not true that the Word was with God and the Word was God (John 1:1)? Is not the name of Jesus above all other names? Jesus is not only the founder of Christianity; he is also the *foundation* of the salvation that God has in store for the whole humanity.

So, if you ask, "Who is this Christ who redeems?" I could hand you a fish, and you would know the answer. The fish was one of the earliest Christian symbols. In Greek the letters that spelled fish—IXTHUS—represented an ancient Christological confession: Jesus Christ Son of God Savior. If a person asks you for a fish, will you give him a serpent (Matthew 7:10)? If you are rummaging around in the wastebaskets of the past, looking for Jesus, minus the names and titles and symbols that speak of his unique saving meaning, you will get a serpent, not a fish.

Does that mean that our Christian faith is built on a fish story? Yes and no. To some the primitive Christian claim seems fishy, the very idea that this Jew—the itinerant rabbi from Nazareth, crucified by Roman soldiers just outside the city of Jerusalem among terrorists and criminals—is today the living Messiah, the risen Lord, and the Savior of the world. Were they not stretching things a bit much, those men and women who left the tomb on Easter morning, huddled in a house on Pentecost, and then virtually sprang upon the world with the good news of the gospel of salvation through Jesus the Christ? They went forth from Jerusalem and Judea to the far ends of the earth, so that even we can say that we have heard the same message and believe the very same gospel. Amen!

5

John and Jesus: A Study in Contrasts

Mark 1:4-11:

> John the baptizer appeared in the wilderness, proclaiming a baptism of repentance for the forgiveness of sins. And people from the whole Jordan countryside and all the people of Jerusalem were going out to him, and were baptized by him in the river Jordan, confessing their sins. Now John was clothed with camel's hair, with a leather belt around his waist, and he ate locusts and wild honey. He proclaimed, "The one who is more powerful than I is coming after me; I am not worthy to stoop down and untie the thong of his sandals. I have baptized you with water; but he will baptize you with the Holy Spirit."
>
> In those days Jesus came from Nazareth of Galilee and was baptized by John in the Jordan. And just as he was coming up out of the water, he saw the heavens torn apart and the Spirit descending like a dove on him. And a voice came from heaven, "You are my Son, the Beloved; with you I am well pleased."

John the Baptist and Jesus of Nazareth were cousins. Both of them came unexpectedly into the world. John's mother Elizabeth was an old woman; she had been barren for many years. Jesus' mother Mary was a virgin; becoming pregnant was the last thing on her mind. John and Jesus apparently grew up without knowing each other. They did not live in the same neighborhood; they did not go to the same school or attend the same synagogue. Most of all, they adopted completely different lifestyles. John headed for the desert and lived in the wilderness. Jesus stayed at home and worked in his father's carpenter shop. John's diet consisted of grasshoppers and wild honey; no bread and no wine. Jesus enjoyed good cooking and ate with his friends, Mary, Martha, and Lazarus. He attended wedding feasts and somehow got the reputation of being something of a glutton and drunkard, as well as keeping company with sinners and other undesirables. Jesus did not call attention to himself by dressing in a weird way, unlike John, who clothed himself with camel's hair and a leather belt around his waist.

Why Was Jesus Baptized by John?

Then Jesus and John met one day at the river Jordan. They had come to know about each other by reputation. This was one of the most significant encounters between two men in world history. John had acquired a reputation of being a "hellfire and damnation" preacher. His message was, "You brood of vipers. Who warned you to flee from the wrath to come? . . . Even now the ax is lying at the root of the trees; every tree therefore that does not bear good fruit is cut down and thrown into the fire" (Luke 3:7b, 3:9). He must have been a very dynamic preacher. Crowds of people from Jerusalem and all around Judea came out to hear him. Shaken to the core, they cried out, "What then shall we do?" (Luke 3:10). He called upon them to repent and to be baptized for the forgiveness of their sins.

Many people began to ponder the question, "Who is this guy anyway? Is it possible that John might be the Messiah?" John the Baptist would have none of that speculation. He possessed the clarity of a true self-understanding. "The one who is more powerful than I is coming after me; I am not worthy to stoop down and untie the thong of his sandals. I have baptized you with water, but he will baptize you with the Holy Spirit" (Mark 1:7-8).

Theologians have puzzled over this question for centuries: Why did Jesus need to be baptized? He was the spotless and sinless Lamb of God who takes away the sins of the world. Unlike everyone else, he had no sins to confess and, therefore, no need of repentance. Why did he enter the waters of Jordan to be baptized? Jesus said, "For it is proper for us in this way to fulfill all righteousness" (Matthew 3:15b). That means, in short, he was designated to carry forward God's plan, to be born of a woman, subject to all the needs, experiences, and temptations of human beings in general. It was God's plan that he should become fully what we are, so that we might become fully what he is, to paraphrase something St. Athanasius said.

Martin Luther referred to God's mission for Jesus as a "happy exchange." Jesus would exchange his righteousness for our sinfulness and our sinfulness for his righteousness. This baptism was an epiphany, the first public manifestation of the true identity of Jesus. As the heavens opened up and the Spirit of God descended on Jesus like a dove, a voice from heaven declared, "This is my Son, the Beloved, with whom I am well pleased" (Matthew 3:17).

John the Baptist knew that he was nobody compared to this special somebody. He announced, "I am the voice of one crying out in the wilderness" (John 1:23). I am the messenger, I am not the message. I am a forerunner; I have come to prepare the way for someone who is infinitely greater than I. John the Baptist was the last in a long series of prophets going back to Moses, Elisha, Micah, and Malachi.

This encounter between John and Jesus is of great significance because it links the Old Testament to the New Testament. Old Testament prophecy comes to an end, and the New Testament age of fulfillment begins. The latter is greater than the former. The Old Testament prophets were great, yes, but the Messiah whose coming they prophesied is even greater. Jesus put it this way: "Truly I tell you, among those born of women no one has arisen greater than John the Baptist, yet the least in the kingdom of heaven is greater than he" (Matthew 11:11). In a sense, that means that any New Testament Christian is greater than any Old Testament prophet, and that's solely because of the infinite superiority of Jesus Christ to all the prophetic messengers and forerunners that preceded him.

A famous altar painting by Matthias Grünewald in Isenheim, Germany, depicts this scene of Jesus meeting John at the river Jordan. Jesus is at the center of the painting, with John standing off to the side. With an outstretched arm, John points a forefinger to Jesus. John got it right, for that is exactly the mission of the prophet, to point to Jesus who is at the center—at the center of world history, of the church, and of the life of every Christian. On another occasion John said to his own disciples, "I am not the Messiah, but I have been sent ahead of him. . . . He must increase, but I must decrease" (John 3:28b, 3:30).

True and False Witness to Jesus

How unlike so many other self-styled prophets and founders of new religions, who believe and teach that they are greater than Jesus. Mohammed taught that Jesus was a great prophet in line with Abraham and Moses, but that he himself was the greatest of them all. His motto was the opposite of John's: Jesus must decrease so that I might increase!

The same goes for other religious founders. Joseph Smith founded the Mormon Church, teaching his followers that the revelation he received from an angel supersedes the revelation of God in Jesus Christ. That makes the *Book of Mormon* more authoritative and definitive than the Old and New Testaments.

The same thing is true of the Unification Church, founded by the Reverend Sun Myung Moon. Moon teaches that Jesus was great but a failure. Whereas Jesus failed to build a paradise on earth and to bring in the kingdom of God, these things would now be fulfilled through the messianic ministry of the Reverend Moon and his followers.

Moon's motto is the same as that of all the messianic pretenders and founders of American cults and sects: Jesus must decrease, so that we might increase. That is what makes a cult a cult and what makes a sect a sect. To be sure, they always reserve a place for Jesus, to fool the gullible, but he always comes in second. Jesus is regarded as just another John the Baptist, preparing the way for the founder of the latest cult or sect. The tragedy is that millions of Americans have been deceived into believing the stories of these cultic and sectarian gurus. They keep on coming and growing on the fertile soil of American religion and culture.

John the Baptist was a good Jew, like his parents Zacharias and Elizabeth. They lived in the Old Testament situation, looking forward to the coming of the Messiah. In spite of their differences, Jews and Christians share a lot of common ground. Both Jews and Christians believe in God the Creator of heaven and earth. Both believe in God's election of Israel as the chosen people. Both accept the Law and the Prophets of the Hebrew covenant. Both believe in the promised Messiah whose coming would redeem Israel and reconcile the world unto God.

Still there is an important difference. The difference is exactly as John the Baptist saw it—the difference between the messenger and the message, between the prophet and the Messiah. Like John the Baptist, Orthodox Jews are still in the Old Testament situation, looking forward to the coming of the Messiah. Christians believe that the Messiah has already come, and that his name is Jesus, the man of Nazareth who was baptized by John in the river Jordan.

Jesus of Nazareth is different from all other religious prophets, founders, and leaders. He is the only beloved Son of God, not one among many. He is the Word of God made flesh, who lived a human life like the rest of us. He declared himself to be the bread of life, the light of the world, the good shepherd, the resurrection and the life. He said, "I am the way, the truth and the life. . . . I am the vine, you are the branches" (John 14:6; 15:5).

Let us pray that we might be like John the Baptist, a witness to the truth of God that arrived in Jesus the Messiah. Let us not follow any other religious leaders, who place themselves above Jesus. Let our motto be like John's: He must increase, but I must decrease. He is the one and only Savior of the world, not one among many. He is the one and only Lord, not one among many. Let us also confess as doubting Thomas did, meeting Jesus after his resurrection, "My Lord and my God" (John 20:28). Amen.

6

Christ Is the Mystery of the World

Ephesians 3:7-12:

> Of this gospel I have become a servant according to the gift of God's grace that was given me to bring to the Gentiles the news of the boundless riches of Christ, and to make everyone see what is the plan of the mystery hidden for ages in God who created all things; so that through the church the wisdom of God in its rich variety might now be made known to the rulers and authorities in the heavenly places. This was in accordance with the eternal purpose that he has carried out in Christ Jesus our Lord, in whom we have access to God in boldness and confidence through faith in him.

Matthew 2:1-12

> In the time of King Herod, after Jesus was born in Bethlehem of Judea, wise men from the East came to Jerusalem, asking, "Where is the child who has been born king of the Jews? For we observed his star at its rising, and have come to pay him homage." When King Herod heard this, he was frightened, and all Jerusalem with him; and calling together all the chief priests and scribes of the people, he inquired of them where the Messiah was to be born. They told him, "In Bethlehem of Judea; for it has been written by the prophet: "And you, Bethlehem, in the land of Judah, are by no means least among the rulers of Judah; for from you shall come a ruler who will shepherd my people Israel.'"
>
> Then Herod secretly called for the wise men and learned from them the exact time when the star had

appeared. Then he sent them to Bethlehem, saying, "Go and search diligently for the child; and when you have found him, bring me word so that I may also go and pay him homage." When they had heard the king, they set out; and there, ahead of them, went the star that they had seen at its rising, until it stopped over the place where the child was. When they saw that the star had stopped, they were overwhelmed with joy. On entering the house, they saw the child with Mary his mother; and they knelt down and paid him homage. Then, opening their treasure chests they offered him gifts of gold, frankincense, and myrrh. And having being warned in a dream not to return to Herod, they left for their own country by another road.

The Meaning of Epiphany

We have read both the Epistle and Gospel texts appointed for the celebration of the Epiphany of Our Lord. Epiphany is one of those days in the church year rather unfamiliar to most Christians. How many people come to church to celebrate the Epiphany of Our Lord? Christmas? Yes. Easter? Yes. But Epiphany? What is this all about?

Epiphany comes from a Greek word that means to "make manifest," to shed light upon a mystery. The Gospel text from Matthew tells about the star that shone in the East and led the wise men to Bethlehem. This was the manifestation, the epiphany, of the child who was born to be king of the Jews.

Mystery is intriguing. People like to read mystery novels. At the end of the story they are relieved when all secrets are disclosed. No religion would be interesting if it contained no mystery. Mystery lies at the heart of every real religion. Some years ago pseudo-prophets were announcing the coming of a secular age in which religion would be obsolete. Supposedly we had reached an era which leaves no room for myth, miracle, or mystery. Everything supernatural or mystical was supposed to have given way to a universal rationality in a global secular culture.

But then came the backlash with the New Age Movement and a plethora of exotic spiritualities. The shelves of today's bookstores are stocked with literature about mystery cults, satanic powers, and secret societies. People seem to be bored with the one-dimensional thinking of a superficial secular scientific mindset.

Not all the mysteries in the universe, however, bear good news. Daily newspapers carry reports about people in high and low places who are driven by mysterious evil forces. King Herod was one of them. He was the pro-Roman king of Israel at the time that Jesus was born in Bethlehem. He was trying to break open the code of prophecy and to read the astrological signs, to locate the exact time and place where the Messiah was to be born, king of the Jews. He said he wanted to pay him homage, but in fact his plan was to kill the baby Jesus. He was running up against God's plan for this baby boy, and he did not know it. From eternity this child of Mary was destined to be revealed some day as the mystery at the heart of the universe. The wise men came from the East to show that this Jewish boy would have universal significance. He would become the bridge between East and West, North and South, and the unifying destiny of everything past, present, and future.

The Mystery of Christ

We celebrate Epiphany as the manifestation of the universal meaning of Jesus Christ. We have here the embryo of the world missionary mandate of the church. This one particular Palestinian Jew is the mystery revealed as God's only way of salvation, not only for the tribes of Israel but also for all the peoples of the world.

In Ephesians Paul speaks of the mystery of Christ. This mystery was given to him to know by a special revelation, not by the scientific study of world religions. He was commissioned to bring the knowledge of the mystery to the Gentiles, the good news of the boundless riches of Christ. This was the deepest mystery hidden for ages in God who created all things—the mystery at the heart of the world. This mystery has been given to the church to make known to all nations.

People wonder, why the church? Do not all religions have equal access to the mystery of God? It would not seem to be fair of God to show such favoritism to one religion. The wise men from the East certainly knew the mysteries of the eastern religions, but they came all the way to Bethlehem to behold the mystery of God lying in a manger. The Star of Bethlehem has in turn led thousands of missionaries to the east, to follow in the footsteps of Paul to make known the eternal purpose of God carried out in Christ Jesus our Lord.

The mission of the church is to reflect the full mystery of Christ in all its rich variety, not to water it down or sugar-coat it to make it easy to swallow. Many trends in today's church and theology have been in mad pursuit of relevance. They have been playing the game of relevance roulette with the mystery of Christ. They have tried to give a psychological interpretation of the gospel—to make people feel good. We have advertised the practical truth of the Christian faith—offering commercials for the "be-happy attitudes" of possibility thinking. Christianity has been recruited to support partisan politics as well as to lend ideological weight to one ism or another: socialism, communism, liberationism, multiculturalism, feminism, conservatism, capitalism—whatever happens to be the politically correct thing at the moment.

Mystery points to reality beyond the limits of reason. Mystery cannot be measured, calculated or controlled by the clock. Academic theology often subjects the texts of the Bible to a system of critical methods that drains away all the mystery, eliminates the myth and the miracles, and thus destroys the meaning of it all.

Confusion in the Church

King Herod tried to kill Jesus. A similar thing occurs whenever we deny the necessity of Christ in our faith and doctrine. Here are some examples:

The first one has to do with the category of religious experience. It is certainly true that there are varieties of religious experience, as William James affirmed—different strokes for different folks. It is no doubt true that at various times people experience moments of ecstasy and transcendence. Perhaps they may even be overwhelmed with serene feelings of peace and unity with the cosmos. Perhaps they experience being accepted by a sacred power greater then themselves and from that derive a sense of wholeness, even of being healed. You see, I am talking the jargon of our age. But what does all that have to do with the good news of the gospel about Jesus? The gospel is Jesus Christ—not our feelings about this, that, or the other thing.

Some time ago I received a brochure advertising a conference for "more effective ministry in the new millennium." It was put out by a group of pastors not many miles from where I lived. It promoted one of the keynote speakers at this ministry conference in these words: She "has long been immersed in the study of creatively gifted, spiritually emerging adults. . . . (She is) one of the foremost exponents of the practical value of self-actualization." Then the blurb offers a quotation from one of her writings, which says: "Spirituality helps us merge our inner experience with that of others. People's spiritual life is linked to whatever fascinates, interests, or engages them. When we touch our deepest fulfillments or gifts and the wonderment of our own unseen energies, we are instantly invigorated. These fulfillments unite us not only with our physical or sensory natures but also with our subtlest inner values and tones of consciousness. The deeper we go into these interior essences, the more strength, health, vitality, and 'is-ness' we absorb."

This kind of rhetorical gobbledygook has nothing whatsoever to do with the great mystery of Christ that was manifest to the wise men that night long ago in Bethlehem. This sort of stuff is pure Gnosticism—the perennial religion of self-actualization—with its talk about inner values, interior essences, and tones of consciousness. It appeared at a ministry conference for pastors because many have apparently lost the art of making a proper distinction between the one great truth—the mystery of Christ—and the fleeting trends that fascinate and engage us.

The wise men from the East already knew about the religion of self-actualization, of being in touch with the unseen energies of their inner selves. But they left all that to go to Bethlehem, to pay homage to a great new mystery revealed in the tiny baby born to be King of the Jews, King of kings, and Lord of lords.

Let me point to a second example of confusion rampant in the church and theology today. One of the cardinal principles of morality and ethics is that passion for justice is a good thing. Justice is an extension of the Golden Rule. It is a good thing for us to have a great passion for justice; it grieves us to see how little justice is meted out to the poor and the oppressed. God calls all human beings to act in solidarity with the poor in quest of political and social liberation; Christians should be in the vanguard of authentic liberation movements. But the Golden Rule is not the gospel. All the causes and crusades to make this world a better place in which to live do not add up to the good news of the gospel.

The epiphany of Christ is not necessary to summon people to fight against injustice and human misery. The Gentiles know about the basic moral imperatives for the good life, even apart from Christ. No doubt we have often marveled how many of our friends who are not Christians display a moral sensitivity equal to and sometimes even superior to that of many Christians. The result of confusing faith in Christ with common morality leads to what theologians call the "social gospel." That leads our hearts and minds away from the mystery lying in the manger of Bethlehem.

Wherever I travel and speak in Christian assemblies of one kind or another, I feel compelled to tell people how disastrous it is for Christians to neglect the great mystery of our religion, as the letter to First Timothy puts it (1 Timothy 3:16), in exchange for some lesser truths about spiritual journeys, psycho-social wholeness, and passion for peace and justice, without any necessary reference to Christ and the gospel.

The gospel can be known and experienced only on its own terms; that gospel is the mystery of Christ, as Paul said. It comes to us only by revelation, not by reason. It conveys the riches of Christ, not the wisdom of the world. The gospel can only be proclaimed by the church; it cannot be found latent in the native spiritualities of religious people.

Otherwise Christ would have been born in vain. Otherwise Christ would not need to have died the death he died for all. Otherwise we would not need to come before God clothed in the robes of righteousness purchased by the blood of his cross.

This one Lord Jesus Christ is the great mystery that we celebrate in this festival of Epiphany. May we, as the wise men of old, come and worship him, the newborn King of the Jews, King of the universe. Amen!

PART TWO

The Spirit and the Church

Ecclesiology is the study of the church, its nature and purpose. Church is an English word that comes from the Greek word *kuriake*, a word related to *kyrios*, meaning "Lord." It is appropriate to deal with ecclesiology in almost the same breath as Christology, because the church is the body of Christ and Christ is the head of the church. The church came into existence because the Holy Spirit created a response to the person of Jesus of Nazareth in the minds and hearts of his first disciples and apostles. To the Jews and the Greeks and the Romans the early Christians confessed that their faith lies not in a set of laws, ideals, or stories but in a person—the person of Jesus.

Nevertheless, to keep its message alive and faithful to its origins, the ancient church undertook a series of crucial historical innovations. It produced the Apostles' Creed, the New Testament canon to add to the Old Testament, an order of service centered in the Lord's Supper, and a threefold office of the ministry—deacons, pastors, and bishops. These four factors defined the Christianity of the first five centuries. A Lutheran preacher of the gospel—as I am—is indebted to Luther's efforts to reform the church of Rome by appealing to the creeds and doctrines of the first five centuries of Christianity because they rightly interpret the Scriptures.

7

The House of God

Ephesians 2:19-22:

> So then you are no longer strangers and aliens, but you are citizens with the saints and also members of the household of God, built upon the foundation of the apostles and prophets, with Christ Jesus himself as the cornerstone. In him the whole structure is joined together and grows into a holy temple in the Lord, in whom you are also built together spiritually into a dwelling place for God.

1 Corinthians 3:16:

> Do you not know that you are God's temple and that God's Spirit dwells in you?

In Jesus' "Sermon on the Mount" the man who hears the words of the Lord and acts on them is like a man who digs deeply and builds his house on a rock. Let us think about the house of God, its foundation, the one who builds the house, its reason for being, and the materials used to build the edifice.

The Foundation

I have recently learned a few things about what goes into building a house. My son is a builder of homes in Chicago. This is how he works: He surveys the neighborhoods to find a lot to buy, then digs the basement, lays the foundation, and builds the house according to the architect's plan.

The New Testament says that is what the Spirit does in building the church, the house of God. It is important that the house be built on a solid foundation. The foundation is invisible. What people see is the house, the façade, the design, and all the creature comforts.

What if the house is built on sand? Before the floods came, it looked just as beautiful as the house built on a rock. You could not tell the difference from outward appearances. But what a difference the foundation makes.

So it is with the church today. Here may be a church with lots of people, growing by leaps and bounds. You can read about it on its website. This is a church that gives people what they want, whatever makes them feel good. This church has everything money can buy, a selection of classes on every popular subject, support groups, child care facilities, clean bathrooms, and entertaining worship. Who can argue with success, quantifiable in numbers—members and meetings, budgets and buildings? One pastor of such a successful, fast-growing church—14,000 members—was asked, "Just how do you do it?" His answer was: "We try to make sure that when people come, they don't leave with the feeling they've been in church." That is exactly what happens. They do not get church; they get Christianity Lite, a religion for consumers. We are talking about a house built on quicksand, not on the solid rock on which the church can withstand every tempest and temptation.

The foundation is hidden but all-important. My son hired a subcontractor to build the foundation. When the rains came, the basement leaked. The contractor had apparently cut corners and did not follow the plans, just to put more money into his pocket. That happens a lot in Chicago, they tell me, but it is also happening in the churches of today. Since the foundation is invisible, maybe we do not need to worry about it. People cannot see it anyway. The main thing is to give them what looks good.

In the Old Testament the rock is the God of Israel. The grand confession of faith in the Psalms rings out: "The Lord is my rock and my salvation." Israel found itself between a rock and a hard place, learning the hard way that either this rock is her ultimate foundational support, or it becomes a stone of stumbling.

In the New Testament the rock of Israel is no longer called by the mysterious name of Jahweh, but by the name of Jesus. Nathanael addressed him: "Rabbi, you are the Son of God! You are the king of Israel!" (John 1:49). Paul says: "For no one can lay any foundation other than the one that has been laid; that foundation is Jesus Christ" (1 Corinthians 3:11). Thus, the rock of Israel is none other than Jesus Christ, the foundation of the church, against which not even the gates of hell can prevail. All who believe and are baptized are supported by Jesus Christ, the way a house is supported by its foundation. A person who finds his or her hope of salvation elsewhere is not a living stone in the household of God, founded on Jesus Christ. The building materials of this house are those forgiven, regenerated, and justified by faith in Christ, and whose lives are a continuous act of worship and witness.

This foundation is not some imagined Jesus, painted in the colors of our own emotions, wishes, and needs. The church's one foundation is the whole Christ of the whole Bible. Paul says that Christians are "members of the household of God, built upon the foundation of the apostles and prophets, with Christ Jesus himself as the cornerstone" (Ephesians 2:20). If we take seriously the rock on which the church is based, then preaching is a living and faithful commentary on Holy Scripture, not a religious discourse, not a medium for the pastor's favorite ideas and experiences, and not cute little stories to tickle the ears of the parishioners. The house of God has no other possibility of existence and survival than to lay claim to this foundation, Jesus Christ, the eternal Word of God, the Word made flesh, alongside of which every other competing authority lures the church, first into blasphemy, then into idolatry. It does not go without saying, and it can no longer be taken for granted, that the churches today in America and Europe are remaining true and faithful to the Rock of Ages.

In the summer time we live in a condo on Lake Geneva, Wisconsin. One summer a strange thing happened. The water main broke under the condo. The experts said that, given that there was no basement, the condo was in danger of sliding off its foundation. I thought about the church: We continue to read shocking stories of church officials and theologians pushing the church off its foundation. Jesus used a figure of speech, how the sheep hear and heed the voice of the Good Shepherd, and run away from the voice of strangers—those thieves and bandits who try to lead the sheep astray.

The Builder

It would be wrong to think that it is our job to build the house of God on the foundation of Jesus Christ. Who is the real builder of the house of God? When Jesus died, there was no church. When Jesus was raised by the Father, there was no church. When he was taken up to heaven to be at the right hand of the Father, still there was no church. The scene is now ready for the descent of the Holy Spirit.

The Son of God who was born from Mary's womb to be the foundation of the church descends a second time at Pentecost to give birth to the church of Jesus Christ. Imagine the apostles trying to build the church prior to Pentecost. Perhaps they might have succeeded in founding a new religion, like a Joseph Smith or a Mary Baker Eddy. They might have founded a cult in honor of a dead hero. No, despite having been disciples for three years, studying at the feet of Rabbi Jesus, they could not have built the church and presented Christ to the world as the foundation of a new and eternal community—because flesh and blood cannot do this, because the faith of the church is miraculously born from the Holy Spirit beyond all human possibility. The Spirit gave the apostles words to speak and gave their listeners ears to hear. The truly impossible happens. The dumb are able to speak the Word of God. Paul humbly admits, with no intent to insult his brothers and sisters, "not many of you were wise by human standards, not many were powerful, not many were of noble birth" (1 Corinthians 1:26).

We are fundamentally in the same situation. We are no more capable of maintaining the church than the apostles were of creating it. Only our incapacity is less apparent, because we are swimming in Christianities of all sorts. What does it matter that the scandal has been taken out of the gospel, that the stumbling block has disappeared into the fog of religious pluralism? Are we not all flourishing anyway?

Every one of the denominations has its own tradition of which to be proud; each one bearing the brand name of its founder or its distinguishing characteristic. But none of that has ultimate meaning. All the solemn assemblies, church-wide conventions, and new styles of ministry are nothing but vain activism without the ecstatic presence and blessing of the Holy Spirit. All of our fondest traditions are nothing but dead letters without the internal testimony of the Holy Spirit, who builds the church on the Rock.

If God does not speak to us in the voice of the Spirit, our words are impotent. We cannot even make a decision for Christ, except as an echo of the Spirit's decision on our behalf who makes us living stones in the household of God.

It is impossible for the Spirit to build on another foundation than on Jesus Christ. No one can confess that Jesus is Lord except by the power of the Holy Spirit. The Spirit does not bypass the Son; the Spirit does not put us into a direct relation to God the Father by going over the head of Jesus Christ. It is time for us to reappropriate the *Barmen Confession* for our time; time to confess the one Word of God, the unique foundation of the church and the only hope of salvation for us and for the world.

You know about the famous quarrel between the East and West over the *filioque*, interpolated into the Nicene Creed by the Latin church. Apart from the politics of it, there can be no question that any church that claims to be orthodox cannot seek to have access to the Father apart from the Son and will confess no other Spirit than the one who builds the house of the Lord on the foundation of Jesus Christ.

We were once dead stones, scattered and isolated. We were once languishing in the valley of dry bones into which the Spirit has breathed new life. We are the building blocks, the construction materials, now living stones in the household of God. The stones are not all the same, not all the same size and shape, nor put in the same place. They are not interchangeable. We are not necessarily the most beautiful stones in the whole building. We are not necessarily closer to the foundation than any others. But each one is important, each one counts, each one has its place, put there by the master-builder.

Consider what Paul says of the body: "If the whole body were an eye, where would the hearing be? If the whole body were hearing, where would the sense of smell be? But as it is, God arranged the members in the body, each one of them, as he chose. If all were a single member, where would the body be? As it is, there are many members, yet one body. The eye cannot say to the hand, 'I have no need of you,' nor again the head to the feet, 'I have no need of you'" (1 Corinthians 12:17-21). The point is, all of us who rest on the same foundation need each other.

It is a scandal that many of our churches, even those that claim to be the most orthodox, act as through they need only themselves, as though all the rest of us get in their way. There are no second class members in the household of God. Paul says, "To each is given the manifestation of the Spirit for the common good" (1 Corinthians 12:7). Do we dare to think that every member of our parishes has been given just as special a place in the house of the Lord as a hand or foot enjoys as a member of our bodies?

The Purpose of the House

What is the purpose of this house? The house is built *on* God, God the Son; the house is built *by* God, the Holy Spirit; and in the third place the house is built *for* God, for the glory of God the Father. The house exists for the glory of the Father. That is its purpose and destiny, its sole service. Is that really enough? Are there not more important things for the church to accomplish? Are we still capable of believing with our fathers and mothers in the faith that the only thing that distinguishes the church from the world is its pursuit to glorify God the Father? Apart from that fact the world can match what the church does at every turn. The church exists for the glory of God. The house is built on the rock of Israel by the Holy Spirit, all for the sake of the glory of God. This means for the church to remain totally unpreoccupied with its own glory.

The devil is always at work trying make us replace the glory of God with the glory of the church itself, the glory of own brand of Christianity. "This people honors me with their lips, but their hearts are far from me; in vain do they worship me, teaching human precepts as doctrines" (Matthew 15:8-9). This sounds like Jesus is talking about us, the contemporary church in many places. It is not easy to resist the temptation to seek glory for oneself, for one's own church, or for one's nation. God is on our side, we hear people saying. We are the good guys fighting the bad guys out there.

A church that exists for the glory of God exists by this very fact before the world and for the world. It is city built on a hill; it cannot be hid. Whoever invented this idea about an invisible church? The church of the New Testament was very visible. An invisible church does not get persecuted. Invisible martyrs do not get thrown to the lions. A person who is not engaged in a visible church is not a living stone in the house of God and cannot live for the glory of the Father.

The world needs a church that visibly renders glory to God and delivers it from all false glory. We must not separate glorifying God in our worship and serving the world, just as we cannot separate the two commandments—love of God and love of neighbor. In other words, the church cannot seek the glory of God without pursuing the salvation of the world—for the two come to the same thing. God is glorified where people glorify him and call upon others to do the same thing, for the God of the church is the Savior of the world and the King of kings.

The church does not have its own private Savior and Lord. The church has a mission to erase the boundary between the church and the world, so that the world might believe, all to the glory of God. That is the missionary attitude of the poor in spirit, who seek the glory of God.

Huge segments of the American church are in deep trouble. They have given up on world mission and evangelization. They have made themselves ripe for re-evangelization. A church that does not evangelize has lost the gospel and has lost its own soul. It is a church of the lapsed.

But thanks to be to God, for he has promised that he will not give up on his church. God is still in charge. Let us not despair; let us not lose hope. God in Jesus Christ is the foundation of the church we cannot shake; God the Holy Spirit is the builder of the church and very much alive; God our Father is the eternal destiny of the church. From him, by him, and for him, one God, Father, Son, and Holy Spirit, three persons indissolubly one. What begins in God cannot but end in God, for he is the beginning and the end, the alpha and omega.

So let us pray, Come Holy Spirit, *Veni Spiritus Creator*! Amen!

After Easter, the Church!

1 Corinthians 15:1-8:

> Now I would remind you, brothers and sisters, of the good news that I proclaimed to you, which you in turn received, in which also you stand, through which also you are being saved, if you hold firmly to the message that I proclaimed to you—unless you have come to believe in vain.
>
> For I handed on to you as of first importance what I in turn had received, that Christ died for our sins in accordance with the scriptures, and that he was buried, and that he was raised on the third day in accordance with the scriptures, and that he appeared to Cephas, then to the twelve. Then he appeared to more than five hundred brothers and sisters at one time, most of whom are still alive, though some have died. Then he appeared to James, then to all the apostles. Last of all, as to one untimely born, he appeared also to me.

A lot of controversy is taking place in virtually all Christian denominations today. The controversy in the end is about the church, its nature and purpose. Confusion abounds concerning what the church is and what it is for. Ecumenical dialogues that have been going on in worldwide Christianity have reached an amazing degree of consensus on the Trinity, Christ, the way of salvation, Scripture and tradition, and even on the doctrine of justification, but when it comes to the church, old differences continue to maintain the divisions.

The behavior of the churches is also the object of much suspicion. Polls indicate that many people profess to believe in Jesus but see no point in belonging to the church. People tend to be very critical of the church, but they love to attend huge religious gatherings—the Billy Graham Crusades, the weekly gatherings in the Piazza of St. Peter to see the pope, the *Kirchentag* in Germany, Promise Keepers—all of these draw huge crowds. Many in the crowds are disillusioned with the church.

To cope with this negative image problem, some churches are trying to look like something else. One church in Phoenix offers a service that has a nightclub feel, where the jazz is hot and so is the rock music. The pastor preaches in khakis and a denim shirt. The pastor says: "The point is to give the young adults and baby boomers, who are freaked out by traditional church, two things: music they can relate to and a relevant sermon." The title of the sermon for that week was, "The Art of Choosing Friends." One of those attracted to this congregation said that he believes in Jesus but the church is a problem, and he wouldn't think of joining one. One Lutheran congregation dropped the word church from its name so as not to turn people off.

The church is carrying so much baggage that creative leaders are trying every stratagem to reconnect with alienated people fed up with the church. The pope himself made headlines when he publicly repented of all the sins of Catholics down through the ages. If he would have listed all of them one by one, he would have run out of breath.

Rather than stir the pot of controversy, I invite you to behold the closest possible link between the church and Easter. What happened after Easter? The church was born. In Paul's First Letter to the Corinthians, he reminded them that he came preaching the good news. They believed and were saved. The good news in a nutshell is that "Christ died for our sins, that he was buried, and that he was raised on the third day." But that was not enough to start the church. The risen Christ had to appear. First he appeared to Mary Magdalene, to Peter, other disciples, to 500 other brothers and sisters at one time, and then he appeared to James and all the apostles. Last of all he appeared to Paul. And *voila*! That was the trigger that led to the formation of the early Christian church. Of course, let us not forget that Pentecost completes the story, with the outpouring of the Holy Spirit. More of this later.

In the appearances of Christ we have the story of the church's founding. If Jesus had not been raised from the dead, no church would have seen the light of day. The synagogue would have carried on business as usual. Without Jesus appearing to the apostles, there would have been no church to tell and retell the story of his death and resurrection.

When we are confused about who we are, it is essential to remember where we come from. When Alex Haley wrote a novel treating the problem of African American identity, he called it *Roots*. When we wrestle with the problem of Christian identity, it is likewise a matter of our roots. Our roots take us back to the resurrection of Christ and his appearance to the apostles immediately after Easter.

Scholars have debated whether Jesus, before his death, founded the church. Did he not gather the twelve disciples around himself, whose mission was to go "to the lost sheep of the house of Israel?" (Matthew 10:6). Did Jesus not preach that the kingdom of God is at hand and call for repentance and faith? Did Jesus not teach his disciples the Lord's Prayer and gather them for table fellowship on the eve of his death? Was that not the beginning of the church? Yes and No. In his life and activity Jesus was sowing the seeds of the kingdom. But it was not until after his death and after Easter morning that the Jesus-movement became visibly the apostolic church under the glare of world history. If the crucifixion had been the end, there would have been no Christian church. Not until after Easter did the first Christians speak explicitly and often of the church.

After Easter the picture became clear that Jesus was laying the foundation stones of the church in his own life and ministry—a community meal, a prayer, a messianic lifestyle of being for others, especially the least and the last, a new understanding of God as Father, and freedom from the straightjacket of religious and moral legalism. In founding the apostolic church, the risen Christ launched the apostolic mission. He said, "Go therefore and make disciples of all nations" (Matthew 28:19). He said, "Go into all the world and proclaim the good news to the whole creation" (Mark 16:15). The risen Christ said, "Repentance and forgiveness of sins is to be proclaimed in his name to all nations, beginning from Jerusalem (Luke 24:47). He said, "As the Father sent me, so I send you" (John 20: 21).

The apostles were witnesses of the risen Christ. They were called and sent on a mission to bring the gospel of Good Friday and Easter to the nations. With Christ as the chief cornerstone, they laid the foundation. As long as they could trust their memories, they would know what to say. But what would happen after all the apostles had died out? How can the church be and remain fully and faithfully apostolic in post-apostolic times? What are the provisions? What are the signs, symbols, and instruments to make that happen across all the frontiers of time and space? Jesus did not tell them. He left some things for the Spirit to do after Easter, after the Ascension, and after Pentecost. But what to do? That was on the agenda of the first seven councils of the ancient church. That was on the agenda at Augsburg in 1530. This is our agenda: How to be the apostolic church, doing the apostolic mission of the risen Christ, not as apostles—because we are not apostles—but as successors of the apostles, as those who come after, taking up where they left off.

In council after council—ever since the first Council of Jerusalem—the church has gathered under the guidance of the Spirit, to make decisions about keeping its faith and mission apostolic. The church was free to be very pragmatic about it and to do new things. Their thinking was: Let us do whatever it takes to strengthen our bonds to the church of the apostles. If it means selecting a privileged collection of writings, let us do it and call it the New Testament. If it means producing a new statement of faith, let us do it and call it the Apostles' Creed. If it means lifting up certain rituals that keep salvation in Christ alone central, let us do it and call them sacraments—Baptism and the Lord's Supper. If it means developing offices of leadership that will preserve the church in the true faith and guard against false teaching, let us do it and call these ministers deacons, presbyters, and bishops, according to their different roles and responsibilities. What the church did was, to be sure, done under the guidance and inspiration of the Holy Spirit. The church was not improvising on its own. The Holy Spirit made sure that the church did what was necessary to keep the church apostolic in post-apostolic times, to keep the faith of the apostles and their mission on track until the end of history and time.

May the Spirit of God grant us the freedom, insight, and inspiration to do whatever it takes to keep the faith and institutions of the church apostolic in these postmodern times. Amen.

9

Rekindling the Flame

Acts 2:1-4:

> When the day of Pentecost had come, they were all together in one place. And suddenly from heaven there came a sound like the rush of a violent wind, and it filled the entire house where they were sitting. Divided tongues, as of fire, appeared among them, and a tongue rested on each of them. All of them were filled with the Holy Spirit and began to speak in other languages, as the Spirit gave them ability.

The Quest for a New Spirituality

We are going to be speaking about the Pentecostal Spirit, the Holy Spirit of God the Father and our Lord Jesus Christ, particularly in contrast to the spirit of our age—the *Zeitgeist*! We will not focus on all the biblical teachings about the Spirit, noting the difference between the Old and New Testaments, nor can we dwell on the history of the doctrine of the Spirit. We will not summarize the church's dogmatic teachings about the Spirit in relation to the Father and the Son, such as we have in the *filioque* controversy between Eastern Orthodoxy and Western Catholicism. Instead, we will focus on the quest for a new spirituality in our time, in our personal lives, in our Christian communities, and even in the wider secular society. Everywhere people are asking whether in the midst of the valleys of our modern society, the dry bones of our traditional spirituality will live again. Many people, young and old, in and out of the church, are confessing: "Our bones are dried up, and our hope is lost; we are cut off completely" (Ezekiel 37:11).

A widespread feeling exists that the traditional forms of Christian spirituality are not working well anymore. Parents are not succeeding in passing on a concrete form of Christian spirituality to their children. We believe that the word itself, "spirituality," refers to something important, even essential, and that is the highest quality of human life. But we are not sure what it is. While the traditional forms of spirituality are not being smoothly and spontaneously transmitted to the next generation, we must boil down the matter of Christian spirituality to its barest essentials, and this at a time when the major trends in our increasingly secularized society threaten to make our lives a spiritual wasteland.

In old-fashioned Lutheran language, we place the whole of life and its interpretation under the light of law and gospel, the two basic forms of the Word of God. In more contemporary language we may say the same thing when we interpret the law as the prophetic power of negation and the gospel as the creative presence of transcendence. Law and gospel, negation and transcendence, two ways of God meeting us in his Word, saying a clear "No" to whatever is contrary to God's will and a resounding "Yes" for the sake of our salvation.

The fiery flame of Pentecost has been flickering in the winds of rapid change. Our task is to rekindle the flame, that is, to recover a concrete spirituality. This calls for two things at the same time, first, a new birth of the spirit of prophetic insight, coupled with the courage of protest, and secondly, a revived sense of spiritual transcendence, a lively imagination that creates alternative visions. Let us elaborate these two points further.

Norman Vincent Peale became famous for writing his book, *The Power of Positive Thinking*. He made his point, and we are wise to keep it in mind. But equally important is the power of negative thinking. Otherwise we become victims of the prevailing spirit of positivism, which accepts the world as it is, surrendering to the objectifying consciousness of science and technology. The power of negative thinking is required for us to hold our heads above the tides of our time. It functions psychologically as a contrast device, pointing out the glaring difference between the world as it is and the coming world of God's kingdom which has a higher right to exist. A spirituality of the concrete spirit is able to stand before oneself and the powers that rule this age and say, "No. Enough is enough! So far and no farther. We won't go along with the trends of the times. We won't bow down to the idols of this age." Such is the power of negative thinking. Nancy Reagan put it simply, "Just say 'No'!"

At its best monasticism was driven by this negative factor in a dynamic spirituality. The desert monks made a dramatic protest against corruption in the world and the secularization of the urban Christians. A common opinion is that the monks were *escaping* to the desert—but not at all from their point of view. They went into the desert to do battle full time against the forces of sin and Satan.

St. Athanasius' *Life of St. Anthony* makes it clear that, at least in Anthony's mind, he was not running away from the battlefield. In that age it was thought that the devils had their headquarters in the desert. Anthony only wanted to go where the action was. He and the other monks entered a life of renunciation, to beat the devil on his own ground. The devil preys upon our desires and appetites; he has us at his mercy when he implicates us in so many activities that we become too busy and overwhelmed to put up any resistance to what is going on in the world around us.

It is a sobering thought of Martin Luther that he prayed the longest and hardest when he had the most to do. In any case, it is important to see in the monastic movement the power of negative thinking, the vital voice of protest against a worldly church that was conforming to the trends of the times, the economy of the world, and the politics of the day.

The spiritual power of negation has been diminished in the totalitarian systems of life, dominating everyone through the mass media, mass education, mass advertising, making plastic minds in a plastic culture that leaves less and less room for those who really say "no" and do not want to be swallowed up into mass conformity. We live in a society that wants to melt us down into one pot in which everyone and everything comes out looking alike. True spirituality is lacking when there is no voice in the wilderness crying the forgotten truth of the absolute worth of each individual soul against the collectivism of our big systems. This is why prayer in quiet moments of solitude is so essential, now more than ever, as a way of becoming free of the babble of voices of the world in the church and of the church in the world, each telling the other what they like to hear.

The loss of true spirituality leads to loss of selfhood; it is called "burn out." The self gets lost in the world of objects, schedules, committees, jobs, and a jillion things to do. The existentialist philosophers (Sartre, Camus, and others) called it dehumanization, depersonalization. This happens to us when we succumb to a one-dimensional world. The world gets flattened into bits and pieces minus the whole, yielding a body without a soul, mammon without mystery, a drama without a plot, a life without a future, sex without love, religiosity without faith, words without meaning, and on and on. A deep prejudice of our culture and education is that non-material things do not exist, that non-scientific statements cannot be true, that what is most visible, measurable, and quantifiable has the highest value. Days fly by, threaded together one after the other on the string of time, leading nowhere, because the chronological calendar has displaced the liturgical calendar in which time becomes sacred time, the passing of time a process of redemption, and history the story of our salvation.

Our spiritual struggle is not against flesh and blood, but against demonic structures with power to destroy humanity. Our mindless technological machine is like a vampire that lives on the blood it sucks from its victims. The problem of spirituality today is how to live a human life in the vacuum of a total structure that uses technology to promote mass-mindedness and materialistic patterns of behavior. Our waking hours and leisure time, our manual activities and mental operations—all are invaded and dominated by hidden mechanisms of persuasion and control, making people lust for what they do not need, all the while leaving unsatisfied the basic human needs of body, mind, and spirit.

The Spirit of Our Age

The Spirit of Pentecost tells us that the value of a human life is infinite and absolute. But the spirit of our age says that life is cheap. The value of a person used to be measured by the work he or she produced. But even the meaning of work is being taken away. Robots can do the job more efficiently. With the loss of spirit, the human being is defined only in functional terms. That spells loss of identity, loss of infinite personal meaning, no more the feeling of being unique, irreplaceable, and non-exchangeable for something else, for someone else.

The rat race in our society causes human beings to collapse of sheer exhaustion, or more literally of broken hearts, as they drive themselves to become the irreplaceable individual that counts for something. This built-in need to be assured of one's uniqueness and infinite worth is something that can only come as a gift and acknowledgment from God. That is what makes us human beings theological creatures. When we do not receive that word of assurance from God, we go to work on our own, to make it by ourselves. That is why we spend so much money glamorizing our personalities, cultivating our individuality, primping according to the latest fashions, looking for some badge of distinctiveness, perhaps even assuming a special combination of non-conforming manners and mannerisms.

In a world that denies us our spiritual God-given uniqueness, we are bound to go searching for our lost identity as infinitely beautiful and non-interchangeable unique persons. But this search for identity and meaning ends in a failure. We cannot do it on our own. It makes a wreck of people who try to retrieve their spiritual center, their personal identity, by pouring their souls into external and superficial marks of uniqueness. The "who am I?" question cannot be answered out of this world, from a worldly point of view. The answer can only come from the Holy Spirit, a Spirit not of this world and not the spirit of the times.

We will appreciate the need for a renewal of the prophetic spirit, the spirit of judgment and protest, the power of negative thinking, once we acknowledge that many of our traditional forms of spirituality are not working. I do not think we can exaggerate the feeling of emptiness and the sheer boredom many people experience in the churches they attend. Many religious institutions are a spirit-less affair, like a barren carcass eaten away by the eroding acids of secularism and relativism. The bureaucracies that run them are like the blind leading the blind. The mountains of material cranked out by the office machines to stoke the ecclesiastical furnace may only be choking off the tiny tongues of spiritual fire coming up from below.

A few years ago people at the grass-roots all over the land were crying out for a new church, a new shape of American Christianity. Yet, lest we allow ourselves to be tempted by cynicism, we should remember the assurance that the living God "has not left himself without witnesses" (Acts 14:17). The Spirit blows where and when it pleases God. And so, having stressed the negative principle in a concrete spirituality, we must now turn to the other side, the experience and celebration of transcendence, the coming of the Spirit of God in the body of our time and history, of our life and community.

The power of negative thinking cannot live off of its own negativity. A sheer "no" is impotent without an underlying "yes" to truth from which it gets the clarity of its prophetic vision. A lie is always living off the truth—like a parasite. Only an honest person can tell a successful lie. Nobody believes notorious liars. The point we are making is that the power of prophetic negation must be allied with the sense of spiritual transcendence. In the logic of Christian spirituality the negative pole is most directly visible and audible, but the quiet sense of transcendence is prior.

As a rule I do not really have the will to say "no" unless my imagination is captured by an alternative vision. The strength of the "no" feeds on the power of transcendence. The early Christians said "no" to the imperial gods because they had been grasped by a new God who was the true God. They could say "no" to the present age because they anticipated the new age that was coming. It was their "yes" to the oncoming future of God's kingdom that freed them to hang loose in the saddle of this present age. It was their faith and loyalty to Christ in the power of the Spirit that was the source of their new lifestyle of refusal—refusal to go along, refusal to get wholly plugged into the imperial pagan system that led to decay, decadence, and death.

The Blowing of the Pentecostal Spirit

The Spirit blows into the present from the eschatogical future of God and his kingdom, taking hold of life in the tension between the powers of the old age and the new. We need to keep in mind the eschatological key to interpret the person and work of the Holy Spirit in the New Testament. The Holy Spirit was experienced in the early church as the presence of the power of the eschatological future that had already appeared in Jesus of Nazareth, God's Messiah for his people Israel and ultimately for all the nations of the world.

The Holy Spirit is the Spirit of Christ, the risen Lord Jesus. The Apostle Paul saw the Spirit as the power of God raising Jesus from the dead. Wherever people confess Jesus as Lord, there the Spirit is active. Everywhere in the New Testament the Spirit is known by his testimony to the living Christ. It is the Spirit who calls and keeps believers in the community of Christ. "For all who are led by the Spirit of God are children of God" (Romans 8:14).

The Spirit is as the Spirit does. The Spirit does what the Father and the Son sent the Spirit to do. The Spirit is the power of unity, integrating believers with each other into the body Christ and binding them with Christ to God the Father. The Spirit can do the work of unity in the world because the Spirit is the power of unity in the reciprocating relations between the Father and the Son. The vitalities of faith, hope, and love in the church proceed from the Spirit of God the Father and our Lord Jesus Christ. At Pentecost the same Spirit who opened the eyes of the disciples so they could really "see" Jesus the risen Lord, now becomes the driving power of the universal mission of hope to the nations.

We need to pray for the rekindling of that Pentecostal flame in the churches today. We have been calling for a concrete spirituality that moves between the poles of law and gospel, judgment and grace, negation and transcendence. Only those born of the Spirit enter into the kingdom of God. It is not enough to say, "Lord, Lord." A true confession of Jesus as Lord is possible only in the power of the Spirit. What did Martin Luther teach us in the Small Catechism?

> I believe that by my own reason or strength I cannot believe in Jesus Christ, my Lord, or come to him. But the Holy Spirit has called me through the gospel, enlightened me with his gifts, and sanctified and preserved me in true faith, just as he calls, gathers, enlightens, and sanctifies the whole Christian church on earth and preserves it in union with Jesus Christ in the one true faith. In this Christian church, the Holy Spirit daily and abundantly forgives all my sins, and the sins of all believers, and on the last day he will raise me and all the dead and will grant eternal life to me and to all who believe in Christ. This is most certainly true.

Luther had the gift of spiritual insight to be able to write such a clear explanation of the third article of the Creed. And we, like the earliest Christian community, pray daily to be filled with the Spirit, so that our word and witness may be like a spreading flame throughout the world.

Rekindling the fame—that means to embody a spirituality of the Spirit of God the Father and his Son Jesus Christ. Such a spirituality will possess concrete meaning, affecting our very own bodies. At times in the Christian tradition, spirituality moved away from our bodies, zooming off into mysticism, gnosticism, or spiritualism. But for the Apostle Paul, the Spirit and the body go together. He said, "The body is . . . for the Lord and the Lord for the body" (1 Corinthians 6:14). He coined the term, "the spiritual body," the *soma pneumatikos*. (1 Corinthians 15:44) A spiritual body is one in which the eschatological future of God is already taking up residence. The body is the temple of the Holy Spirit. True Christian spirituality does not leave the body behind. The Spirit is bringing the power of Christ's resurrection into this dying world and into this concrete piece of the world that is our body. The body, not something else, is the battlefield of the two opposing power systems, each struggling to take hold of a person's life.

Christian spirituality is not the ascent of the soul out of our bodies, but the descent of the Spirit into our bodies. We need to get into the spiritual struggles of our age with our bodies. The body is the key to a vital Christian spirituality. All the fullness of God inhabited a human body, the body of Jesus. God is Spirit, to be sure, but we never meet the Spirit of God outside our bodies. We are members of the body of Christ. The salvation we are offered by grace is the redemption of our bodies (Romans 8:23). The renewal of spirituality will begin with the body as the concrete locus of the Spirit. When the flame is rekindled in our bodies today, we will know it by its fruits: a new vitality, a new sense of freedom, a new sense of peace, and a new sense of transcendence. All of this is happening in our bodies, open to the Spirit of God, who still has something new say to the church of our time. Amen!

PART THREE

Evangelism and Mission

The question of Christian identity is being asked with a new sense of urgency because of the resurgence of other religious options everywhere in the world. England is rapidly becoming a Hindu nation. Germany and France are both experiencing tremendous growth of the Muslim population. North America has provided a hospitable home to virtually all the religions of the world. Christianity no longer holds a monopoly in Europe and America.

Meanwhile the commitment to evangelize the nations has gone flat in the mainline Protestant denominations. Nowadays, few who call themselves Christian or belong to the churches think of Christianity as a dynamic force to change anything in the world, let alone convert people of other faiths to Jesus Christ.

Preaching Christ today must grapple with the question of the proper approach of Christians to people of other religions. These sermons aim to reaffirm the classical Christian conviction that the gospel is a unique message of salvation in a religiously plural world.

10

Evangelism:
The Heart of the Church's Mission

Acts 4:12:
> There is salvation in no one else, for there is no other name under heaven given among mortals by which we must be saved.

The Biblical Mandate for Mission

We believe and confess that Jesus Christ is the one and only Savior of the world, of all peoples, nations, cultures, and religions. We literally believe what the apostle Peter preached in Jerusalem, that there is salvation in no other name. This belief is the springboard of the worldwide mission of the Christian church.

If there is salvation in some other name, say, in the name of Moses, Buddha, Muhammad, or Krishna, there would be no need for Christ, the preaching of the gospel, and the global mission of the church.

But, of course, this one verse does not stand alone. The whole story of the Bible, all the promises and events declared in the Old and New Testaments, convey the singular truth that God has accomplished the salvation of the world in Jesus Christ.

The church has received a mandate from the Lord Jesus to carry this saving truth to all people. It is that simple. We do it because Jesus commissioned his people to "go into all the world and proclaim the good news to the whole creation" (Matthew 28:15). But not only to go and preach, but to baptize and teach—in the name of the Father and of the Son and of the Holy Spirit.

The apostolic pattern of going into the world follows that of the incarnation of God's only begotten Son, as the Gospel of John gives it classical expression: "As the Father has sent me, even so I send you" (John 20:21). Advance signs of this model of "sending and going" can be seen in God's election of his people Israel. God called and sent Abraham, commanding him to go from his home country into a place and a future unknown. God sent Joseph into Egypt, God sent Moses on a mission to liberate Israel, and he sent a long line of prophets to declare his promises to the chosen people. Finally, "when the fullness of time had come, God sent his Son, born of a woman, born under the law" (Galatians 4:4). And, that we might enjoy the freedom of the children of God, "God has sent the Spirit of his Son into our hearts, crying, 'Abba! Father!'" (Galatians 4:6). No longer slaves in bondage to the law, we are free, free at last.

God has revealed to us his eternal secret concerning the good news of the mystery of Christ for the salvation of the world. The church is part of God's secret plan of salvation, an essential part of God's delivery system, to make known the good news to all the nations. St. Paul wrote, "But how are they to call on one in whom they have not believed? And how are they to believe in one of whom they have never heard? And how are they to hear without someone to proclaim him?" (Romans 10:14). All members of the church are called to bear witness to the full and final revelation of God reconciling the world unto himself in Jesus Christ.

The Missionary Heritage

We have sketched, citing a few passages, the basic biblical mandate for the mission of the church. The whole Bible sounds forth a clarion call to Christian mission. We are concerned about the statistically evident lukewarm response of the mainline churches and congregations to the Great Commission of our Lord. Lutheranism began as a confessing movement, as a call for the pure preaching of the gospel. Lutheranism at its beginning was not a missionary movement. That came later with the revival movement of the Pietists in Germany and Scandinavia. Lutheranism is historically both a confessing movement and a missionary movement—those are the two great rhythms of our living tradition.

From the period of Lutheran Orthodoxy we have inherited a centripetal concern for the pure doctrine of the gospel, an inward-looking vigilance for the sake of the pure preaching going on in the church. That means we are a confessing movement that lives to renew and inform the whole church by the gospel of justifying faith through Jesus Christ alone.

From Lutheran Pietism we inherited a centrifugal passion to traverse the whole world, to cross the frontiers of faith and the barriers of unbelief. That means we are a missionary movement that exists to proclaim the gospel to those who have never heard, and to plant new churches in lands and among people who do not know Christ, who do not experience the benefits of his saving grace.

As Lutherans we are a confessing movement and we are a missionary movement, both at the same time, or we are nothing but a dying relic of a religion that has lost its heart of faith and courage to act.

In Luther's Large Catechism we read this explanation of what we mean when we pray in the Lord's Prayer, "Thy kingdom come."

> This we ask, both in order that we who have accepted it may remain faithful and grow daily in it and in order that it may gain recognition and followers among other people and advance throughout the world. So we pray that led by the Holy Spirit, many may come into the kingdom of grace and become partakers of salvation, so that we may all remain together eternally in this kingdom which has now made its appearance among us.

Then the explanation concludes: "All this is simply to say 'Dear Father, we pray thee, give us thy Word that the gospel may be sincerely preached throughout the world.'"

The preaching of the gospel is still going on throughout the world. Yet some who call themselves Christians believe or act as though we have come to the end of the missionary era. In fact, some of Luther's most zealous followers, claiming to be orthodox, taught the silly notion that the apostles had fulfilled the command of Christ to take the gospel to the whole world, so all we need to do is to hang on and remain faithful.

Lutherans have a great missionary heritage. They have fused the marks of their confessional identity with their evangelistic activity. Lutheran missionaries have planted churches in many parts of the world. The young churches in Asia and Africa have learned to speak the confessional language of the Lutheran tradition, and often the members of these daughter churches are more faithful in their struggles than many of us in the older mother churches. In world evangelization Lutherans bring a treasury of evangelical principles that we would be derelict to squander away in faithlessness and negligence. Consider what we have to share with our ecumenical partners in mission:

1. The principle of *grace alone* makes clear the unconditional gift of God's love in Jesus Christ. This means that the mission of the church is not born out of its own generosity; it does not stem from its own altruistic initiative. Instead, its sole source lies in God's free decision to act graciously in behalf of humanity and the world.
2. The principle of justification by *faith alone* says that human beings cannot achieve the righteousness God requires to measure up to the standards of his holy will. Being made right with God, becoming justified in the sight of God, is a gift that can be received only by faith, and cannot be brought about by any amount of good works of religion or morality.
3. The principle of *Christ alone* means that God has identified himself finally and supremely with the person of Jesus of Nazareth, so that he is the sole Savior of the world, the only Mediator between God and humanity.
4. The principle of *Scripture alone* means that the Bible is the sole source and standard by which we can judge the definitive truth of God's Word in Jesus Christ. There is no other part of the church's tradition that can be put on a par with the sacred writings of the Old and New Testaments.

The Evangelistic Priority of Mission

Those are the principles that should keep us on the straight and narrow path of God's mission in history; they determine the priorities of our church's agenda. The Holy Spirit of God the Father and our Lord Jesus Christ created the church to serve the world by carrying the good news of the crucified and risen Christ to all persons and peoples. This is the unique task of the church; no other agency can do it; no other institution cares about how the gospel is doing in the world. It is therefore imperative that the church make the gospel of God its number one priority and not exchange its glorious birthright for a mess of worldly pottage.

Everyone incorporated into the body of Christ through faith and baptism is called and commissioned by the Spirit of God to bring the gospel of the kingdom to all who do not yet believe. The church is to do this to the ends of the earth and till the end of time. As Matthew says, "This good news of the kingdom will be proclaimed throughout the world, as a testimony to all the nations; and then the end will come" (Matthew 24:14).

The mission of the church is orchestrated to be on schedule with God's eschatological timetable. We do not know exactly the times and the seasons, but we do know that the church has a part to play in God's plan of salvation, according to his eternal mystery and hidden wisdom. One cannot find out about this plan by reading the editorial columns of *The New York Times* or the *Chicago Tribune*. It is the church's secret.

The ordinary Christian knows more about the meaning and destiny of all God's creatures than the mightiest rulers of nations and empires, because Christians confess that all things are moving toward their future end and will stand in the light of the glory of God when Christ will judge the living and the dead. Until this plan is consummated, until all the promises of God have been fulfilled, the church must be perpetually on the move in the power of the Spirit to bring the name of Jesus into the mother language of every person whose sins Jesus bore on the cross and of every sinner sick unto death for whom God raised Jesus from the grave.

The church is a pilgrim people on the way to the nations, encountering people of other loves and loyalties. What shall we do when we meet these people? So many are uneducated, so many hungry, oppressed, poor, wretched, victims of war and violence, humiliated by prejudice and brutality. It makes your stomach ache; it makes your heart break. We cannot ignore the call of Christ to the ministries of mercy, to help alleviate pain and suffering, to lift people out of their miseries, and to liberate people from ignorance, poverty, and oppression. Indeed, we must not neglect the diaconal works of mercy and compassion.

The apostles were not content to devote themselves to prayer and serving the word of God; they saw to it that the widows would be cared for. So they appointed seven deacons to the task of waiting on tables. Today, the tables are very large and often empty, and the daily distribution of food is a staggering assignment. Our Lord himself indicated that the signs of the kingdom are in view when "the blind receive their sight, the lame walk, the lepers are cleansed, the deaf hear, the dead are raised, the poor have good news brought to them" (Luke 7:22). The love of God is total, reaching out both to poor people and poor sinners. It is not a matter of choosing one over the other.

Missionaries have taken a bad rap, criticized for preaching the salvation of souls while neglecting their physical needs. This criticism comes from people with an evil spirit who do not believe in the gospel of eternal salvation that the missionaries preached. The great mission societies started schools, taught literacy, built hospitals staffed with doctors and nurses, fed the hungry and clothed the naked. I know this, not from reading books but from seeing with my own eyes, how the missionaries in Madagascar, including my father, Torstein, and mother, Clara, stretched their capacities to the limit in trying to meet every spiritual and physical need they encountered. As a boy I remember how every morning scores of poor, hungry, and sick folks would squat on the mission compound waiting for food, clothing, and medicine, which my mother distributed to each one.

The missionaries had their priorities straight, and today the exploding continent of Africa is reaping the harvest of the seeds of the gospel that the missionaries sowed two and three generations ago. It is ludicrous to hear today's mission bureaucrats criticizing the missionaries of yesterday, while they jet around the world attending conferences on mission and evangelism, staying in posh hotels, eating in fancy restaurants, talking about dialogue with people of other faiths, always comfortably at room temperature.

For many among the Christian intelligentsia, dialogue has become a substitute for evangelism. Dialogue is no sweat, no scandal, and no shame. It is elegant, polite, and civilized, always conducted in an atmosphere conducive for academicians. I have had my share of it. My disenchantment is not with the idea of dialogue; I believe in it. It is always so much better when people of different religions talk to each other rather than kill each other. But often the enthusiasm for dialogue carries the high price tag of discounting what is most central in the Christian faith—the necessity of Christ, the tri-unity of God, and the absolute truth of the gospel. Today dialogue has become virtually a code word for syncretism, relativism, and pluralism, isms that betray the uniqueness and finality of Jesus Christ.

A Christ-centered evangelism will always drive us onward to meet people of other religions in conversation and dialogue. Do not get me wrong. Dialogue is a good biblical concept and practice. In the book of Acts, St. Luke used the word "dialogue" nine times to describe how Paul did not only preach, but also reasoned, argued, persuaded, and discussed with people who did not yet share his belief in the gospel. I believe in that kind of dialogue. Call it apologetics. So whether in evangelism or in dialogue with persons other than Christian, Christ remains the flaming center and our commitment to the apostolic imperative keeps us motivated.

Implications for Gospel Mission

In recent years there has occurred a sharp reduction in the number of dollars and missionaries committed to the church's global mission of evangelization. Just when this is happening, the new theology tells us that everything the church is doing is mission, even collecting money for the pension fund. How can we lose? How can we not succeed in mission, when by definition everything we do as a church is called mission. Ecumenical relations, college and seminary education, peace and justice advocacy, multi-cultural ministries, inter-religious dialogue—these are all very good and important things. Where does that leave evangelism, the one thing that gives meaning and motivation to all the other activities of the church? The danger is that world evangelization becomes buried in an avalanche of church activism, under the management of burgeoning bureaucracies.

Evangelism is the heart of the church's mission. The heart is not the only organ of the body, but without the heart pumping blood into all the others, the body goes dead. The occupational hazard of *talking* about rather then *being* about the evangelistic task strikes the church at its most vulnerable center. While the church has increased its preoccupation with all sorts of studies and projects of this-worldly significance, each one perhaps worthy enough in itself, the church has decreased its total commitment of resources to what she alone as the church can do, and what no other organization in the world is equipped to do, and that is the task of evangelizing and discipling the nations, to preach and teach the gospel to one hundred million neo-pagans in America and four billion people who have never heard the gospel.

Christians are one-fourth of the world's population, called and commissioned to proclaim the gospel by word and deed to the three-fourths of those who have never heard. The opinion is commonly held that the basic evangelistic task has already been accomplished with the establishment of local churches on every continent. That suggests that we can leave the responsibility for evangelism to the local churches in their contextual settings. This idea bears a family resemblance to the old orthodox view of missions in the seventeenth century, which held that the age of missions ended with the death of the last apostles.

Not so long ago world mission strategists got themselves all geared up to fight communism around the world. Now communism is all but dead. But a more insidious enemy of the gospel has crept up behind us—the neo-pagan culture of Western Europe and North America that is tolerant of Christianity on condition that we admit that Christ is not the only way of universal salvation, that there are many ways, all equally true and saving. Such a condition is no longer hidden away in the fine print of academic speculation. The pluralistic hypothesis is fast becoming the emerging consensus of official documents in liberal Protestant denominations. Instead of calling for a "re-evangelization" of neo-pagan Europe and America, we are swimming in a culture of relativism that holds that all religions boil down to the same thing, merely different loaves of the same "bread of life."

The zeal for overseas missions is not lively in our seminaries. We are training pastors to fill the vacancies of existing congregations and to maintain the institutional status quo. The overseas mission policy of the church is largely a process of negotiating projects of church aid, to dig a well, to fund a radio program, to support theological education, and so forth—again all very good things to do. But what is lost is direct person-to-person witness, face-to-face evangelism. As a result of the loss of the personal dimension, local congregations begin to lose interest, and the zeal for world evangelization diminishes proportionately. Global mission policy is following the trend of the bureaucratic age, in both church and society, thus cutting congregations, pastors, and lay folks out of the action.

It is time to reverse the direction in mission policy, which is backed by a faulty theology. It is time to get back to pioneer evangelism, to the sending of apostolic emissaries whose primary calling is the verbal proclamation of the gospel. It is time to get back to starting new churches, gathering believers into assemblies of worship and witness.

Where there is no vision, the people perish. American churches have greater resources than ever before, in money and people, but they are doing less and less in world evangelism and mission. As Americans in mission we have become paralyzed by guilt. We have internalized the "ugly American" self-image. We have interpreted the nasty calls of "Yankee—Go home!" to signal "Missionary—Go home!" The apostles never waited for a friendly invitation from Rome. Missionaries who have embarked on a career of foreign service for life have come home after serving a term. We have allowed our American consciousness to prevail over our Christian commitment. We have associated ourselves with attitudes of Western colonialism, imperialism, racial superiority, and cultural arrogance. So we have pounded our chests, crying "*Mea culpa, mea culpa, mea maxima culpa,*" using guilt-feelings as an excuse to cop out of the biblical mandate for mission.

If the United States government can find idealistic young people to join the Peace Corps for service in the most primitive of situations, there is no doubt that the churches of America could recruit, train, and support a corps of youthful and adventurous volunteers for missionary work. Instead, most of the men and women studying for ministry dream of getting a call back home, to be close to their families and relatives, enjoying the flesh pots of air-conditioned parsonages and Monday night football. Jesus said something about the cost of discipleship, that whoever does not hate father and mother, wife and children, brothers and sisters, cannot be a disciple of his. "Whoever does not carry the cross and follow me cannot be my disciple" (Luke 14:27).

We are called to do mission under the sign of the cross, modeled on the form of the suffering servant. Like Christ himself, the power of the church in mission will be manifest in weakness, humility, and suffering, not in the abundance of professional skills, technological gadgets, and creature comforts. Our American style of mission is pricing us out of the market. We do not need to adopt the worldly ways of seeking success and growth. The church is not to seek its own glory in the present age, for now "we suffer with him so that we may also be glorified with him" (Romans 8:17).

No matter what the global climate may be, no matter how chilly the weather in international relations, no matter how adversely the social, economic, and political conditions conspire against us, the church still has the indispensable task of witnessing to the ultimate meaning and goal of human life in Jesus Christ, giving each individual a sense of absolute personal worth in the eyes of God. Witnessing to all persons concerning the hope of eternal salvation through faith and the forgiveness of sins is the inalienable priority of the church's mission.

Let us pray God to make us faithful in mission, directing all our energies in the way of Jesus Christ. We have been asked only to plant the seeds and to leave the harvest to God. Amen!

11

No Other Gospel!

Matthew 28:18-20:
> And Jesus came and said to them. "All authority in heaven and on earth has been given to me. Go therefore and make disciples of all nations, baptizing them in the Father and of the Son and of the Holy Spirit, and teaching them to obey everything that I have commanded you. And remember, I am with you always, to the end of the age."

We are living in an ecumenical age. Some churches that have been long separated are merging with each other. The quest for Christian unity has been gathering momentum ever since the Second Vatican Council. In the words of Matthew Arnold, we are living between two worlds, the dying of one and awaiting the birth of a new. As we merge our various ethnic traditions, we confess that we harbor mixed emotions. We are saying "goodbye" to our cozy corners and warm huddles. We have come a long way from our village experience in Lake Wobegon, where we all belonged to a church with people mostly of our own kith and kin. Swedes and Finns and Danes and Germans and Norwegians—we all went to churches of our own kind. Now the basket is upset, and we find ourselves commingling with Blacks and Hispanics and Vietnamese and Native American Indians, like never before.

A Deadly Dilemma

After World War II we experienced a tremendous expansion of Christianity in America and around the world. Professor Kenneth Scott Latourette of Yale University wrote in his monumental *History of the Expansion of Christianity*: "In 1944 Christianity was affecting more deeply more nations and cultures than ever before.... In 1944 Christianity was molding the religious life of mankind as never before.... Never has Jesus been so widely potent in shaping world history as in 1944."

Not many historians would write like that today. The fact is that the steeple casts its shadow over less and less of the western hemisphere. The arts have lost their Christian inspiration; Christian morality has been eroded; and many of Europe's great cathedrals are filled with empty pews.

In America religion has become a consumer product, a leisure-time activity, appealing more to the impulses of the flesh than of the Spirit. It goes in for cheap ecstasy and instant gratification. The Saturday newspaper carries ads for Sunday's services, touting entertainment, uplifting singing, and exciting music. You are invited to get away from the muggy conditions and worship in an air-conditioned sanctuary. Another will advertise that you can worship in your car, or bring a lawn chair for Saturday evening services in the park.

A lot of religious razzamatazz is giving Christianity a bad name. The question we face is: where are we heading? We face a deadly dilemma. The sociologist of religion, Peter Berger, says that the church has two main options: either accommodation or retreat. We can find our niche in America in one of two ways: either by becoming relevant to what is going on in the world and lose our distinctiveness, or retreating into the past and lose our relevance. That is an unacceptable choice.

Either do like the liberals and say "*Gesundheit*" every time the world sneezes. That means to blend into the world and join the passing parade of fads and fancies. This is fast becoming the dominant trend in mainline Protestant Christianity. Make some easy alliances with the world. Some do it to the right and others to the left; either way the world sets the agenda and calls the shots. Or do like some conservatives who wrap themselves in the traditions of the past, like the scribes and the Pharisees of old. They have a siege mentality, building strong defenses against the world. Perhaps our temptation is to swim back into our safe denominational fjords.

American Christianity has always been hung up on this deadly dilemma between modernists and fundamentalists, liberals and conservatives. As Lutheran Christians we are evangelical Catholics of the Augsburg Confession. That makes us neither liberal modernists nor conservative traditionalists, but confessors of the living voice of the gospel in all our liturgical assemblies, bearing the cross of Christ on the front lines of our missionary encounters with the world.

Two Instructions of Jesus

We have the onerous task of escaping the horns of this deadly dilemma. We can do it by opening our minds to the mandate of our Lord to the church. We have two great instructions from Jesus, both of which we must keep together. The first is the Great Commission of our Lord.

> All authority in heaven and on earth has been given to me. Go therefore and make disciples of all nations, baptizing them in the name of Father and of the Son and of the Holy Spirit, and teaching them to obey everything that I have commanded you; and remember, I am with you always, to the end of the age (Matthew 28:18-20).

That is the evangelistic instruction of Jesus. Go, teach, and baptize . . . preach the gospel, make disciples, and reach out to all the nations, in the name of the Holy Trinity. That is a gospel absolute which we dare not relativize to accommodate the religious pluralism of our time, or to make false peace with the idols of this age.

The second instruction of Jesus is the Great Commandment, in two parts:

> You shall love the Lord your God with all your heart, and with all your soul, and with all your mind. . .and you shall love your neighbor as yourself (Matthew 22:37, 22:39).

Only by holding the Great Commission and the Great Commandment together can we avoid the sin of separating our Godward faith and our neighborly love, of separating our world of experience into public and private segments, leaving our church artificially grounded on the private shoreline. The public sphere then drifts off on its own course, and the private sphere appeals only to the "habits of our hearts."

As a church we are engaged in a fierce struggle to maintain the double thrust of world evangelization and constructive social action. Sometimes it seems as though the church is made up of two types of Christians—those who believe in doing good works to help our neighbors improve their life and those who believe in saving souls from eternal fire and damnation—as though the lordship of Jesus covers only half of this world, the half that concerns our souls, the private self, the interior life, our eternal destiny; as though the Lordship of Jesus does not cover the other half, the half that concerns the body, the public sphere, our everyday secular business, and our temporal responsibilities.

A recent exchange of letters between a church official and a seminary professor has been made public. They are very instructive and disturbing, epitomizing the dilemma we are facing—how to be faithful as Christians to the eternal gospel, while as citizens we take sides in the struggles and conflicts of peoples and ideologies in our time.

This seminary professor writes to accuse the church official of taking an ideological pilgrimage to Central America, of using his office to promote his own political opinions on current affairs, of spending the church's hunger funds that should go to feed hungry people, and of elevating the penultimate issues at the expense of the ultimate issues that his office ought to attend to back home.

The church official answers that we cannot separate the ultimate and the penultimate, that the church must not remain silent concerning the moral issues confronting the human family, that the church's mission is always hindered by Christians remaining silent in the face of the many abominations in our common social and political life, some of them even threatening the survival of civilization and possibly of the human species. Did not Christians remain all too silent during the abomination of slavery? Did not the bishops and other church leaders look the other way during Hitler's rule of Nazi Germany and its mistreatment of the Jews?

It would be easy to jump to the support of either the professor or the official and debate the merits of their respective arguments. But for now, let us take it as a sign of the polarization that churches are experiencing at this crucial time of our history.

The Open Door

Our Lord speaks, "Look, I have set before you an open door, which no one is able to shut. I know that you have but little power, and yet you have kept my word and have not denied my name" (Revelation 3:8). To meet the challenges posed by our cultural and religious context, let us walk through the open door. It is a narrow door opening unto us. Let us walk in the living traditions of our fathers and mothers.

Let us go together with the gospel, as the apostle Paul defines it for us. "For I handed on to you as of first importance what I in turn had received: that Christ died for our sins in accordance with the scriptures, that he was buried, and that he was raised on the third day in accordance with the scriptures" (1 Corinthians 15:3-4).

We need to center the church in that gospel truth. John F. Kennedy captured the imagination of the American electorate with his campaign slogan: "Let us get America moving again." Similarly, let us get our confessing movement of the gospel going again. Emerging from our ethnic captivities, we have become open to many things—from the ecumenical movement, the liturgical renaissance, the historical-critical method, and various liberation theologies. Without endorsing everything associated with those contemporary movements, we have learned a lot from them. We thank God for all the gifts from other traditions that enrich our experience, expand our horizons, and make us act more critically and constructively.

But would you agree that perhaps our passion for the gospel, for the one thing needful, needs to be rekindled? Of all the things that the Spirit of God spoke to the seven churches in Asia, in the book of Revelation, the one that I dread the most to hear is what the Spirit said to the church in Laodicea: "I know your works: you are neither cold nor hot. I wish that you were cold or hot! So, because you are lukewarm, and neither cold nor hot, I am about to spit you out of my mouth" (Revelation 3:15-16).

Those are frightening words of judgment, placing us under the full weight of God's law. They tell us to preach the gospel with clarity and conviction, in all its depth and fullness. "And if the bugle gives an indistinct sound," said St. Paul, "who will get ready for battle?" (1 Cor. inthians 14:8). They tell us to preach the message with authority, lest we suffer from what the prophet Amos called "a famine . . . of hearing the words of the Lord" (Amos 8:11).

The one who threatens to spit the lukewarm church out of his month goes on to say, "I reprove and discipline those whom I love. Be earnest, therefore, and repent. Listen! I am standing, knocking; if you hear my voice and open the door, I will come in to you and eat with you, and you with me" (Revelation 3:19-20). Amen!

12

The Gospel and Religious Pluralism

Acts 4:11-12:
> This Jesus is
> "the stone that was rejected by you, the builders;
> it has become the cornerstone."
> There is salvation in no else,
> for there is no other name under heaven
> given among mortals
> by which we must be saved.

In Wilmette, Illinois, there is a beautiful Bahai temple that expresses the belief that all religions point to the same ultimate reality. The temple is built with nine magnificent porticoes, each dedicated to the prophet of one of the world religions. The porticoes provide access to a single central altar via nine aisles, like spokes of a wheel around a hub. The altar symbolizes the one God at the center of the many religions. It does not matter which portico one enters or down which aisle one goes, they all end up at the same place.

The Bahai temple is an architectural expression of the widespread belief that, though the religions seem to be different, they are essentially all equally valid ways to the same truth and salvation. This is no longer simply a tenet of the Bahai or some other sect. This belief is at home in American culture, given our democratic sense that all are equal. But now this "pluralistic theory of religions"—that is the name for it—is making alarming headway within Christian circles—mission boards, church seminaries, and parish pulpits.

The Pluralistic Theory of Religion

Religious pluralism is both a fact and a theory. It is a sheer fact that Christianity is merely one among many religions. Christianity was born in the maelstrom of a variety of Jewish, Greek, Roman, and Oriental religions. Christianity began as a missionary encounter with other existing religions and philosophies, struggling to proclaim the revealed truth of God to all. At first it was attacked by the Jews as a heresy, persecuted by the Roman authorities as a seditious movement, ridiculed by the Greek philosophers as a contemptible myth, and given a run for its money by the popular cults and mystery religions.

There is nothing new about Christians encountering a world with a plurality of religions. What is new is to find Christians adopting a theory or theology that holds that all religions are equally true and saving.

Diana Eck, a professor of world religions at Harvard University, has written beautifully about her spiritual journey from "Bozeman to Banaras," telling how she acquired from her Methodist upbringing in Montana a strong faith in God, a sense of what constitutes the church, and a commitment to the work of the church in the world. Years later she found herself in India, at a Vaishnavite temple where she "beheld the beauty of the Lord" in the peaceful face of Vishnu, praying with her Hindu friends before the statue of Vishnu. She asks, "Was our god the same God? Frankly the question did not occur to me. I simply took it for granted."

The Exclusive Claim of the Gospel

Same God? Same gospel? Tell it to the apostle Paul, who warned the Corinthians about those preaching a different Jesus or the Galatians about turning to a different gospel. Or tell it to Peter who said to the scribes and elders in Jerusalem:

> This Jesus is the stone that was rejected by you, the builders; it has become the cornerstone. There is salvation in no one else, for there is no other name under heaven given among mortals by which we must be saved (Acts 4:11-12).

Many similar passages in the Holy Scriptures boldly proclaim "No Other God!" and "No Other Gospel!" The saving revelation of the triune God is centered in Jesus Christ alone. There is no getting around the exclusive claim of the gospel. But what do the pluralists do with it? They explain it away as an example of parochial attitudes in ancient times or simply reject it as a belief incompatible with enlightened thinking of today.

The first Christians knew that their faith embraced Truth with a capital T, not *a* truth, one among many, but *the* truth, the final Truth of

God for the salvation of the world in Jesus Christ. The New Testament and the Christian Creed present Jesus not as *a* son of God, but as the *only* Son of God, not as *a* savior, but as *the* Savior, and not as *a* lord, but as *the* Lord. These exclusive designations of Jesus as Lord and Savior are part of the kernel of the gospel, not so much husk that can be stripped and thrown away.

The "one and only" statements about Jesus in the New Testament were counter-cultural, not merely a product of the religious outlook of primitive times. The early Christians were ready to place their lives on the line to confess that Jesus is Lord and Savior in an utterly unique sense. They were not merely campaigning to have the blessed name of Jesus included in a pantheon of the world's divinities.

No basis exists in the Scriptures and the Christian faith for the pluralistic theory of religions. Its origins can be found in philosophy and religions other than Christian. About one hundred years ago a young Hindu reformer, Swami Vivekananda, came to the West proclaiming the message that for 2500 years India had already accepted a philosophy of religious pluralism.

Hindu pluralism is illustrated by the famous fable of the elephant and the blind men. Six blind philosophers make an inquiry into the nature of the elephant. One falls against its side and thinks the elephant is like a wall. A second feels the tusk and thinks the elephant is like a spear. For the others, the trunk is like a snake, the leg is like a tree, the ear is like a fan, and the swinging tail is very much like a rope. Each of the great world religions thinks its experience of the mystery of ultimate reality is the truth, not realizing how partial and inadequate it is. Along comes the superior wisdom of Hinduism that knows and teaches the real truth of the matter -- each of the religions teaches truth, one-sided as it is. Their only mistake lies in believing that its partial perspective is the whole truth, that its relative grasp of reality is absolute.

The pluralistic theory of religions is akin to the Hindu view. It claims to possess wisdom higher than any one of the religions. Like the storyteller of the parable of the elephant and the blind men, the pluralist knows that all religions are groping to be in touch with ultimate reality, though each uses a limited metaphor to describe the nature of the great mystery. Christians use Jesus, Muslims Mohammed, Buddhists Gautama, etc. Pluralists believe that is as it should be, so long as the religions do not blindly claim their particular experience to be the universal truth. Only the pluralists know the universal truth, namely, that all religious truths are relative. Their higher insight into the common essence of all the religions is the absolute truth.

Dialogue No Substitute for Evangelization

There is a correlation between the rise of the pluralistic teaching and the collapse of world evangelization. Why evangelize, if all peoples are equally blessed by the same God at work to save through the great variety of religious rituals and experiences? The best we could expect of a church acting on the pluralist vision is a mission of dialogue for the sake of a cross-fertilization of ideas. Evangelization is the hard work of missionaries who preach the gospel and plant new churches. Inter-religious dialogue has become a fashionable substitute, usually carried on politely by academicians at some exotic place to which they have purchased round trip tickets.

Of course, there is a need and a place for dialogue among people of different religions. The religions are often at the root of conflict and violence between warring factions. There is a need for greater tolerance and respect for people of other loyalties—national, cultural, and religious. But this does not mean that Christians should march down one of the aisles to the high altar dedicated to someone other than God the Father of our Lord Jesus Christ. There is salvation in no other name. There is no other gospel for the world's salvation than that preached by the apostles and all those loyal to their faith and doctrine.

General Revelation in the Religions

There is another side of the story that needs to be told. The apostle Paul entered into dialogue with the Epicurean and Stoic philosophers of Athens. Standing in front of the Areopagus Paul said:

> Athenians, I see how extremely religious you are in every way. For as I went through the city and looked carefully at the objects of your worship, I found among them an altar with the inscription, "To an unknown God." What therefore you worship as unknown, this I proclaim to you. The God who made the world and everything in it, he who is lord of heaven and earth, does not live in shrines made by human hand. . . . Indeed, he is not far from each one of us. For "in him we live, and move, and have our being," as even some of your own poets have said (Acts 17:22-24, 27b-28).

This shows that the exclusive claim of the gospel of salvation through Christ does not deny that God has revealed something of his "eternal power and divine nature . . . through the things he has made" (Romans 1:20). Salvation is one thing, revelation another. Not all revelation is saving revelation. The law of God is revealed, but only the gospel saves.

Some theologians distinguish between general and special revelation, or between natural religion and revealed religion, or between law and gospel. The gospel is something extremely particular; it can be appropriated only through faith in Christ. The law, to the contrary, is very general; it can be found everywhere in the world of nature, history, society, conscience, and religious experience.

Revelation is like a broad highway that runs through all the religions. Salvation is a narrow path that starts with God's call of Abraham and proceeds by way of a column of events that includes the election of Israel, the death and resurrection of Jesus, the outpouring of the Spirit, the creation of the church, the apostolic mission to the nations, until the Lord returns in glory at the close of the age. There is simply no way to generalize those particular events into a universal theory of the religions, without losing what is distinctively biblical and Christian, lying at the heart of the gospel. Nor can the gospel be reduced to an abstract religious idea or ideal that lies hidden in the symbols of other religions.

The profound theological reason to be interested in the place of Christianity among world religions is the Great Commission of our Risen Lord—to go and tell the gospel to all who do not yet believe. This is where Christianity came upon the scene of world history in the first place. Otherwise it would have remained a dinky Palestinian sect long since forgotten. The early Christians, though weak and few, dared to take on the world, so convinced were they that the eternal truth, power, and love of God and his coming kingdom had arrived in the person of Jesus, and it was their calling to tell the world about it.

The first Christians were Jews. As such they confessed the one God of Israel. But now they found themselves also confessing Jesus as Lord, whom the God of Israel exalted by raising him from the dead. What? A second God? Here they were calling on the name of Jesus in worship, still claiming to be monotheists in worshipping the one God of Israel as the Father of Jesus Christ. Their prayers and their preaching associated Jesus of Nazareth with God the Father in way that gave rise to a new confession of God as Triune. Jesus told them to go and make disciples of all nations and to baptize them in the name of the Father and of the Son and of the Holy Spirit. This name is unique. It cannot be found in any other religion. We have this name on the authority of Jesus, who claimed that all the authority in heaven and on earth had been given to him.

The Final Hope of Salvation

Pluralists feel that laying so great a stress on the uniqueness of Christ leaves no chance for the salvation of non-Christians. But they miss the point of the gospel. What is unique about Jesus is his universal meaning. This is the beauty of the gospel! Now we have reason to hope, not only for ourselves, but for others, for all! Jesus is not only my personal Lord and Savior; he is the Lord and Savior of the whole world. Even some orthodox Christians believed that somehow Socrates, Plato, and Aristotle would be saved along with Abraham, Isaac and Jacob, and along with Peter, James, and John. How to bring that off has been a subject of mind-boggling speculation. No consensus exists in the Christian tradition on how things will turn out in the end.

The possibility of salvation of those who have not heard the gospel in their lifetime is ultimately a mystery that we cannot unveil by speculation. Will God offer them a "second chance" on the day of judgment? We do not know. Meanwhile, it is good for us to pray that God's will be done, knowing from the gospel that God would have all to be saved and come to the knowledge of truth. God alone is the final judge. God is free from any constraints external to his gracious will. Meanwhile we can trust that God's final judgment will be both loving and just. Amen!

13

God Made Manifest

Ephesians 3:2-6:

> For surely you have already heard of the commission of God's grace that was given me for you, and how the mystery was made known to me by revelation, as I wrote above in a few words, a reading of which will enable you to perceive my understanding of the mystery of Christ. In former generations this mystery was not made known to humankind, as it has now been revealed to his holy apostles and prophets by the Spirit: that is, the Gentiles have become fellow heirs, members of the same body, and sharers in the promise in Christ Jesus through the gospel.

Since the day of Epiphany always falls on January 6, and therefore rarely on a Sunday, it is one of those festivals on the church's worship calendar that easily gets neglected. On January 6 we are still recovering from the excessive celebrations of Christmas and New Year. Besides, there is no great event in the life of Jesus, such as his birth, baptism, death, resurrection, or ascension, that gets commemorated on the day of Epiphany.

Epiphany Means Manifestation

Epiphany means "manifestation." It is based on the story told in Matthew's Gospel of the wise men who came to Jerusalem, led by a star, to look for the child born King of the Jews. This child is God manifest in a baby. He is not only King of the Jews but is also destined to become the Lord and Savior of all the nations. Tradition has it that these sages represent the three races of humankind—black, white, and yellow—in other words, all the peoples, nations, religions, and cultures of human history.

When the baby Jesus became an adult, he offered himself on the cross for the sins of the world. After his resurrection the risen Christ launched the apostolic mission. He said, "Go and make disciples of all nations." He said, "Go into all the world and preach the gospel to the whole creation." The risen Christ said, "Repentance and forgiveness of sins should be preached to all nations," and he commissioned the apostles to be his "witnesses in Jerusalem, in all Judea and Samaria, and to the ends of the earth." That was the beginning of the Christian missionary movement, making the epiphany of God in Christ the central subject matter of world history. From then on the whole of history would be dated with reference to the coming of God in Christ. Even unbelieving historians who teach secular history talk about things happening either B.C. or A.D.

You know the old question: "If a tree fell in a forest, and no one was around to hear it, would it make any noise?" If God became manifest in the person of Jesus, and there was no one to believe or proclaim it, would there by any Christianity, would there be any church? Would God's epiphany in the infant Jesus be a truth to tell to the nations?

One of the saddest facts is that many modern Christians no longer believe we have a story to tell to all the nations, no longer believe that the epiphany of God in Christ is universally valid, and no longer believe in preaching Christ as the Lord and Savior of all humanity, of all religions and cultures. Some modern Protestant theologians—and a few Catholics too—say that every religion has its own deity and savior figure, and that it is none of our business to impose ours on them. Who are we to be so arrogant as to believe that we know the way of salvation and that only Jesus is the "way, the truth, and the life" or that "there is no other name under heaven given among mortals by which we must be saved?" The modernists say that Jesus may be my personal Lord and Savior, but that is only a matter of personal taste. To each his own.

My father and mother were missionaries to Madagascar. They worked among the Malagasy people, doing what St. Paul did in Corinth, Ephesus, and Rome. They preached the gospel of the coming of God in Christ. They worked to propagate the faith and plant the church. Now millions of Malagasy people believe in Christ and belong to his church, members of the same body as you and I. I remember coming home to America, a senior in high school, and one of my aunts said to me, "I can't understand why Clara and Torstein (my parents) would leave America and go so far away. Those people are perfectly happy in their own religion." Of course, I knew that was not true. They are not happy in their religion. They are afflicted not only by poverty, disease, and ignorance, but also by the demons of fear, superstition, and witchcraft. The message the missionaries brought gave them a new way of living and hope for life beyond the grave.

The consequence of thinking like my aunt has been the collapse of the world missionary movement in the mainline churches. Mainline Protestant churches are not sending many missionaries any more. We are leaving that to others—the Pentecostals and Southern Baptists. We seem to have become perfectly satisfied in our own religion, to keep it to ourselves, and no longer desire to do the apostolic thing, to "turn the world upside down" for the sake of Christ and the gospel.

Faithful in Mission

Thinking like that is not thinking like a Christian should. It is not being faithful to the Bible. It is not faithful to Christ or the apostles who laid the foundation of the church, with Christ being the chief cornerstone. If the first Christians would have believed that Jesus is only one of the great prophets, there would have been no gospel mission to the Gentiles. Paul would have kept on making tents. My father and mother could have stayed home in beautiful America, rather than sail to that primitive island off the southeast coast of Africa. Norwegians would still be worshiping Thor, their god of thunder, and Germans would still be offering horse meat to their god Wotan on the Godesberg.

No, Christianity began with the belief that its message is for all the nations. The story of the wise men bringing their gifts of gold, frankincense, and myrrh tells us that whatever truth there is in other religions around the world, they will in the end all come and bow down before the God made manifest in this little Jewish boy Jesus, and render him homage and service.

The early Christians dared to take on the world, not because they were so powerful, not because they were so intelligent, and not because they were so numerous and influential. They simply felt compelled by the truth to go and tell the gospel and make disciples of all nations, teaching and baptizing them in the name of the Father, and of the Son, and of the Holy Spirit. It was the eternal truth of the power and love of God that drove them to action, Truth with a capital T, not a truth, just one among many. The absolute Truth is that Jesus is the final answer, not a savior in the temple of Bahai, one among many, but the one and only Savior of the nations, and therefore very God of very God, exactly of one being with the God of Israel.

The Truth of God in Christ has proved to be a costly truth. To believe and practice it has cost the lives of numerous martyrs. Who would wish to be a Christian and practice the faith at so high a risk? But they did. The church lived, multiplied, and spread throughout Europe, Africa, and Asia. And at last, in these latter days, Christianity has become the most universal of all religions. Its sacred book—the Holy Bible—is translated into more languages and dialects than any other piece of world literature. The church exists on every continent and in every country. We are a part of this world-expanding movement. And now it is spreading into China, where not so longer ago it was thought that Communism had extinguished the flame of the gospel.

Today we are called to carry on in the spirit of Pentecost, to obey the Great Commission of our Lord in our time and place. But it is not easy. We have the opposite problem of the first apostles and early Christians. We are many and strong, we are rich and prosperous, more so than any people in the history of civilizations that Arnold Toynbee has recounted. But we are drowning in our affluence and benumbed by our creature comforts. We are afraid of losing our number one position; we do not dare to risk our good fortune. It is not easy to be leaders of the gospel mission to the nations. It is easier to go with the flow, to blend with the worldly culture around us, and to join the passing parade of newfangled fads rather than stick to the Christian basics of apostolic faith.

But our Lord has not given up on us. We hear his voice calling us to be faithful and true. Again and again he opens doors for the gospel, which no one is able to shut. The doors are opening around the world for Christian evangelists and teachers and nurses and doctors to go with the gospel, to reach out to all people with the life line of salvation. The invitation of our Lord is extended to all who confess Jesus as Lord and Savior.

We have the promise that the gates of hell will not prevail against the church and that the final victory belongs to Christ. In our lifetime Hitler tried to extinguish Christianity and to kill all the Jews. Stalin tried to get rid of Christianity and make it illegal to practice the faith. The communists in Eastern Europe and China closed the churches, killed the pastors, burned the Bibles, and condemned to the Gulag those who believed. But Christianity survived in the hearts of many people. Today the churches have reopened by the thousands, and millions of people, young and old, are flocking to worship God made manifest in the Child of Bethlehem.

We want to be a part of the renewal of the Christian mission around the world and at home. It is the most exciting thing we can do for the rest of our lives—to dedicate ourselves to the cause of Jesus and the mission of his coming kingdom. It is God's design for the world. We have been chosen to be a part of it. Thanks be to God and may his glorious name be praised forever and ever. Amen!

14

The Coming of God in Human Flesh

John 1:1-14:

> In the beginning was the Word, and the Word was with God, and the Word was God. He was in the beginning with God. All things came into being through him, and without him not one thing came into being. What has come into being in him was life, and the life was the light of all people. The light shines in the darkness, and the darkness did not overcome it.
>
> There was a man sent from God, whose name was John. He came as a witness to testify to the light, so that all might believe through him. He himself was not the light, but he came to testify to the light. The true light, which enlightens everyone, was coming into the world.
>
> He was in the world, and the world came into being through him; yet the world did not know him. He came to what was his own, and his own people did not accept him. But to all who received him, who believed in his name, he gave power to become children of God, who were born, not of blood or of the will of the flesh or of the will of man, but of God.
>
> And the Word became flesh and lived among us, and we have seen his glory, the glory of a father's only son, full of grace and truth.

The first words of the Bible are: "In the beginning." The first words of John's Gospel are: "In the beginning." The latter is not the same beginning as the former; it is a new beginning. The book of Genesis in the Old Testament tells about the beginning of creation and the covenant of God with his people Israel. The Gospel of John in the New Testament tells about the new creation and the covenant of God with the church of Jesus Christ. The last book of the Bible—the book of Revelation—goes on to tell about the ending of all things, the final consummation, the great transformation, when God will be all in all.

The Living Word

Meanwhile we are living between the times—the time of the beginning and the time of the ending, between the alpha and the omega, between the beginning of all things and the ending of all things. What is going on in the meantime, here and now in the course of world history? We are centered in the Word of God who became flesh at the mid-point of history, in the person of Jesus of Nazareth. This Word is the bridge connecting the heavenly majesty and glory of God with the earthly flesh and blood of a fallen and sinful humanity. This Word crossed the canyon-like chasm between the infinity of God and a finite world, uniting in his person the divinity of God and the humanity of man.

John's way of capturing the essence of Christianity in words was precisely this: "In the beginning was the Word, and the Word was with God, and the Word was God." By this Word everything in the world was created. Now in the midst of time the eternal Word of God became a human being, entering into the flux of human events. This is the fundamental truth on which Christianity stands. It is the very foundation of the gospel. As Christians we live and die by this Word. Luther said that the church is a "mouth house." The church lives from the Word of God, from listening, hearing, and heeding the voice of God. We have this Word in earthen vessels. In becoming flesh God communicates in human language, with all the riskiness that entails. God might have chosen some other way, but he chose to speak to us in human terms.

From the beginning God used speech to get things done. At the dawn of creation God said, "Let there be light," and there was light. God said, "Let us make man in our image and likeness . . . male and female he created them" (Genesis 1:26-27). And that was done. The God of the Bible is a talking God. Now in these last days, it says in the letter to the Hebrews, "he has spoken to us by a Son" (Hebrews 1:2).

Even when God speaks, speech is a risky business. We live in a culture that is hard of hearing. True, we have hearing aids. We have libraries, more books and magazines, more Ph.D.s and experts, more tools and techniques, to help us get our messages and meanings across. But still ours is a culture hard of hearing. There are several reasons.

First, we have become bored by an excessive barrage of words. Martin Heidegger, a German philosopher, lamented the mass production of counterfeit language by which all the mighty institutions of culture do their business. The politicians, the mass media, the talk shows, the tycoons of industry, and the churches too, specialize in words, but with less and less public trust. We hear of credibility gaps, cover ups, and spin meisters—all of which contribute to the growing suspicion of the powerful wordsmiths of our culture.

Second, people feel that words have become impotent. They say something like, "What's important is not so much talking the talk as walking the walk." They ask for deeds not creeds. Actions speak louder than words, and so forth. Karl Marx said, "The philosophers only interpret the world; the point is to change it." While many will not agree with Marx's formula for changing the world, still, people are tired of empty promises and pious lies. The point is to change what is wrong, not to use words to deceive or to sanction the status quo.

Nevertheless, we have this treasure—the Word of God—in earthen vessels, no matter how deaf the culture, no matter how poisoned the wells of human communication. The reality is this: The Christian faith has no future apart from the living voice of the gospel. Paul asks: "But how are they to call on one in whom they have not believed? And how are they to believe in one of whom they have never heard? And how are they to hear without someone to proclaim him?" (Romans 10:14).

The living Word is Christ himself who proclaims himself through sermons and sacraments in the power of his Holy Spirit. All that we do in worship is a response to the initiative of the living Word. We live and move and owe our being to the living Word for three reasons.

The Mission of the Word

First of all, the mission of the Word is to liberate us from ourselves and our own hang-ups—to get us to look beyond ourselves. That is what we need from pastors—to bring us a message not of our own making and not of this world. The truth of this Word made flesh, now really present to us through audible and visible words, does not arise out of our own experiences. The living Word does not encounter us through transcendental meditation or other self-generated spiritual exercises. It is a Word that comes to us from outside of ourselves. Luther said it is always an external word (*verbum externum*), the opposite of the mystical descent into the soul. Luther said the living Word is an acoustical affair;

someone has to stick it into your ear. What makes baptism a sacrament of salvation is not the water only, but water with the Word. In the sacrament of Holy Communion the bread does not become the body of Christ and the wine does not become the blood of Christ apart from the spoken words instituted by our Lord.

Second, the mission of the Word is to be our adversary. Strange thought—that we should need an adversary. Don't we have enemies enough? Do we need another harping voice, to accuse and beat us down? The truth is, we do need to hear the righteous criticism of the Word of God to cut away our pride. We do need to hear the accusing voice of the law and commandments of God, to bring us to our knees in humility with a penitent heart. No person can be good, no team can achieve excellence, no assembly of sinners can become a communion of saints without sharp and stirring criticism from a master teacher. The Word of God is a two-edged sword, both law and gospel. The goal of preaching is not merely to make us feel good or to soothe our feelings. The mark of the false prophet is to cry "Peace, peace," when there is no peace.

Third, the mission of the Word, in addition to bringing the searing truth of judgment and criticism, is to bring forgiveness, life, and salvation, and to perform the miracle of making us believers in Jesus Christ and members of his church. This is the positive, freeing, healing, and life-bestowing function of the Word of God. This is the loving, caring, and consoling Word, the good news that overcomes all the bad news that the daily headlines throw at us. This is the word of resurrection that brings us a living hope in face of our having to die.

It is the task of every member of the congregation to sit up and listen, to safeguard the pure preaching of the Word and the right administration of the Sacraments. The laity have the responsibility to make sure that the ministry of the Word is free and unconstrained by any worldly ideology —from the left or right—and uncontrolled by loyalty to any external organization, no matter how patriotic or politically correct it may be.

Let us resolve to perk up our ears, to hear and to heed the voice of the living Word of God who became flesh so that he could become the sole mediator of eternal salvation to all who believe and obey. At times it may be difficult to remain faithful and single-minded. We may have to swim against the stream when many around us resort to gimmicks that promise instant success and quick results. Our role as a congregation is to keep open the channels of preaching and teaching and, like John the Baptist, to prepare the way of the Lord and make his paths straight. In doing this we will join that great cloud of witnesses who have gone before. There can be no greater aspiration, no greater achievement for us as a congregation than to be faithful servants of Christ and stewards of God's mysteries. Amen!

PART FOUR

Reformation and Ecumenism

Martin Luther had no intention of founding a new church. His reformation began by merely disputing the selling of certificates of indulgences to raise money to build St. Peter's Cathedral in Rome. The last thing he wanted was to have a church named after him. Yet, contrary to the intent of Martin Luther and Philip Melanchthon, their reforming movement led to a schism that has kept the Western branch of Christianity divided for almost half a millennium.

When Luther dug deeply into the Scriptures, he stumbled upon a verse in Paul's Epistle to the Romans: "The one who is righteous will live by faith." Therefore, heirs of Luther's Reformation treated the doctrine of justification through faith alone apart from the works of the law as the article by which the church stands and falls. This doctrine has now become ecumenical teaching. In 1989 in Augsburg, Germany, Lutherans and Catholics signed a "Joint Declaration on the Doctrine of Justification by Faith." Mutual agreements with other denominations followed suit.

What is the future of the Reformation in an ecumenical age? We believe and confess that the basic truths of the Reformation are perennially valid, framed by the classical three *solas: solus Christus, sola gratia, sola fide*. These sermons aim to point the way to overcome the division of the church and to spell out the implications of this newly achieved common confession for the Christian life.

15

Shadows of the Cross

1 Corinthians 2:2:
> For I decided to know nothing among you except Jesus Christ and him crucified.

I have chosen one verse from St. Paul's First Letter to the Corinthians, as the text for this sermon on Reformation Day. It is a Bible verse that Martin Luther came back to again and again. Church historians and polemicists have bequeathed to us many conflicting images of Luther. For centuries Lutherans have made Luther into a hero, not surprisingly since he was the founding father of world Lutheranism, now numbering over sixty million adherents. Then there is the other side of the story. To Roman Catholics Luther has traditionally been viewed as a rebel who split the Catholic Church, called the pope the Anti-Christ, and was rightly excommunicated. Which image of Luther is historically the more accurate one?

Socialists have derided Luther as a nasty, bourgeois man who called upon the German nobles to put down the peasants' rebellion. In a heat of rage Luther screamed the words, "Stab, slay, and smite those murderous hordes fomenting an armed rebellion." A few historians have portrayed Luther as the spiritual ancestor of Hitler. Luther urged the authorities to take swift and decisive action against the Jews—to burn their synagogues, raze their homes, seize their prayer books, and as a "final solution" send them back to the land of Israel. Indeed, there are so many conflicting images of Luther; the most embarrassing ones we would like to forget.

However, I do not believe that Luther the man as such is a fit subject for a sermon, and Luther would be the first to agree with that. We will leave the question of the real Luther to the historians to debate. Rather, I would like to cut to the chase and focus on the permanent validity of Luther's witness to Christ and his cross.

A New Way of Doing Theology

Luther called for a new way of doing theology. Luther was by training and vocation a professor of the Bible. As a twenty-five-year-old student, Luther wrote in a letter that "the only theology of any real value is what penetrates the kernel of the nut and the germ of the wheat and the marrow of the bone." After he nailed his ninety-five theses to the door of the castle church in Wittenberg (1517), he travelled to Heidelberg to hold a disputation with his fellow Augustinian monks (1518). There he asserted: "The only theology of any real value is to be found in the crucified Christ"—a clear echo of the verse we read from 1 Corinthians 2:2: "For I decided to know nothing among you except Jesus Christ and him crucified."

For Luther the only theology true to the gospel is what he called a "theology of the cross." He contrasted that to a "theology of glory" that was being taught in all the schools at that time. Popular theologians, not unlike many modern ones, were trying to get to God through a variety of other ways, teaching that people can come to know God through philosophy, mysticism, and morality, by means of reason, religious exercises, and good works. All of these ways lead heavenward to a glorious God of majesty, a God who wouldn't be caught dead on the cross of that afflicted man of sorrows, in whom there was no "form or comeliness" (Isaiah 53:2).

Luther was a follower of the apostle Paul's theology. Luther said: There are two ways of doing theology—the way of the philosopher Aristotle who defined God as the First Cause of all things, an absolute who could not care less about what is going on in the world; and then there is the way of the apostle Paul who decided to know nothing except Jesus Christ and him crucified. The two ways of doing theology are the way of glory and the way of the cross. The way of glory rises up to meet God at the level of God in heaven. The way of the cross looks for God in a down-to-earth manner, in things that are as lowly, weak, poor, and naked as the suffering man who died on a hill outside the gate.

God in the Flesh

The cross of Christ involves not only the death of a human being, one Jesus by name. Rather, it is a God-event. The person dying on the cross is not a mere man; he is God in the flesh. This equation results in a strikingly new concept of God. The very idea that God would allow himself to be crucified among criminals—it's unbelievable! The great religions of the world teach that God cannot suffer; God cannot bleed; God cannot die. Because God is God he has no feelings at all; he has no passions; he has nothing in common with the suffering of human beings, in sharing their anguish, despair, and sickness unto death. What happened to Jesus on the cross was something that presumably happened to Jesus only in his human nature. This is what the theologians of glory taught, in order to exempt God from human deprivation and degradation.

For Luther the reformer and Paul the apostle what happened on the cross happened to God. It is right to say that God himself is crucified, because Jesus is not only man but also God. The crucified Jesus is "very God of very God." That is exactly what the Creed of Nicaea also says. God is hidden in the cross of Christ. Theologians of glory flee from the hidden and crucified God in favor of the omnipotent God of majesty. Ashamed to find God on the cross of Christ, their pride tells them to look for God in loftier places, in peak experiences, in which people scale the heights of their own human potential, their reason, creativity, and imagination.

What do we normally think of when we think of God? Do we think of power, glory, wisdom, and majesty? Of course, that is one way, the broad way, but Paul chose the narrow way, where God meets us on the cross of Christ. Let us listen to some of Luther's own words:

> We Christians must know that unless God is in the balance and throws his weight as a counterbalance, we shall sink to the bottom of the scale. . . . If it is not true that God died for us, but only a man died, we are lost. But if God's death lies in the opposite scale, then his side goes down and we go upward like a light and empty pan. But God would never have sat in the pan unless he had first become a man like us, so that it could be said: God is dead; here in Christ is God's passion, God's blood, God's death.

Such a theology of the cross is revolutionary in the history of religion. When it comes to the nature and attributes of God, we are to think about Jesus Christ and him crucified.

Four hundred and fifty years later, Dietrich Bonhoeffer, the martyr who died on Hitler's scaffold, was saying the same thing as Paul:

> God allows himself to be edged out of the world onto the cross. God is weak and powerless in the world, and that is exactly the way, the only way, in which he can be with us and help us. . . . Only a suffering God can help.

The Jewish writer, Elie Wiesel, in his book *Night*, tells about an incident at Auschwitz:

> The SS hanged two Jewish men and one youth in front of the whole camp. The men died quickly, but the death throes of the youth lasted for half an hour. "Where is God? Where is he?" someone asked behind me. As the youth still hung in torment in the noose after a long time, I heard the man call again, "Where is God now?" And I heard a voice in myself answer: "Where is he? He is here. He is hanging on the gallows. . . ."

Could he perhaps have been thinking of the suffering God who humbled himself and became obedient unto death, even death on the gallows?

Only in Christianity do we find this idea that God and the gallows go together. In other major religions, God is high in his heaven and far away. We humans are supposed to go there on the wings of our own reason and experience, our religious rituals and good deeds. Against this Luther said, "We should not try to penetrate the lofty mysteries of God's majesty, but we should simply be content with the God on the cross. Anyone who tries to find God outside of Christ will find only the devil."

The Happy Exchange

Of what use is this theology of the cross for you and for me? In his Letter to the Romans, Paul answers this question by expounding his doctrine of justification by faith apart from the works of the law. The cross of Christ and justification by faith are not two separate things; they are two sides of the same coin. Without the crucified Christ there can be no justification of sinners in the sight of God. In the Lutheran tradition, the doctrine of justification has been called "the article by which the church stands and falls." In light of this doctrine of justification, Luther found much to criticize in the church and theology of his day, from the pope in Rome to the peddler of indulgences in his parish. He claimed that they were teaching salvation by the merits of works and not by faith in Christ and the benefits of his cross. "As soon as the coin in the coffer rings, the soul from purgatory springs." So said John Tetzel, the popular preacher, while selling certificates of indulgence to raise money to build St. Peter's Cathedral in Rome.

What is so great about this salvation that we receive through faith alone on account of Christ alone? What hangs in the balance is the issue of bondage or freedom. Freedom is the very essence of salvation. In his wonderful treatise *On Christian Freedom,* Luther wrote: "A Christian is free . . . and in bondage to no one." Yet, at the same time, he said, "A Christian is a servant, and owing a duty to everyone." Radical freedom was purchased for us by the cross of Christ, and it means to be in bondage to no one, yet free to serve everyone.

The righteousness of God is revealed from heaven. It is not something we render to God but what he gives to us. "Lord Jesus," cried Luther, "you are my righteousness, just as I am your sin. You have taken upon yourself what you were not and you have given to me what I was not." This is what Luther called the good news of the "happy exchange." God in Christ takes our sin, and we get his righteousness. We are free, free at last, and off the hook. Justification by faith alone means freedom from the way of works, which requires us to sweat for every inch of our stature in the face of God. The cross is God's way of shattering the way of works to make way for faith. That is to let God be God who is in the business of saving sinners. This frees us to receive his salvation as a gift and to live life to the hilt.

Luther wrote a letter to his friend, Philip Melanchthon, who was worrying about a dilemma: If he did what he felt he had to do, he would be committing a sin, no matter how hard he tried to avoid it. Then Luther said to his friend, *"Pecca fortiter,"* which means, "Sin boldly!" Go ahead and do what you have to do, and then he added these words of qualification, ". . . believe in Christ even more boldly still, for he [Christ] is victorious over sin, death, and the world." Luther was assuring Melanchthon that Christ did not die for fictitious sinners, but for real sinners. If it were possible for humans to be perfect on their own and avoid all ambiguities, then Christ would have died in vain.

Living Under the Cross

Finally, we must ask, what is the meaning of the cross for the daily life of ordinary believers in the world? The cross is not only a way to be saved but also a way to live. Jesus said, "Take up your cross and follow me." To be a Christian is not only to believe in Christ but also to follow Jesus. To follow him where? Into the world in solidarity with the least, the lost, and the last.

The cross is not a symbol for pious people meditating on things religious. The people of Christ live their lives under the cross, in school, on a farm, in a family, in a business, at city hall, in the everyday secular world, doing what needs doing at the moment. That will sometimes entail suffering, humiliation, grief, disgrace, and maybe even martyrdom. Not many of the disciples or apostles died of old age. Bearing the cross of Christ aroused conflict and opposition. Christians ought to expect that they may be dealt with as sheep for the slaughter. In Greek the word "martyr" is the same as the word "witness." Martyrdom means being a witness to the truth, willing to pay the price that one unavoidably pays in doing hand-to-hand combat with forces of evil in the world.

We confess in the Nicene Creed, "We believe in one holy catholic and apostolic church." Those are the four marks of the true church of Christ. Luther placed on the par with these four marks the additional mark of the cross, of suffering, and martyrdom. A church that wants to be great and glorious in worldly terms, that wants to be vocal and victorious in political terms, is deeply suspect. Something is profoundly wrong with any church that wishes to be identified with the rich, beautiful, and powerful people. That is the way of the theology of glory. The church seeking glory tends to worship its own growth, success, popularity, and to peddle cheap grace to those who can afford to pay their way.

The reason that the Christian life under the cross brings suffering is that those who are set free by Christ go into the world to set the captives free. That means to work for the liberation of the captives, to widen the range of freedom in every respect—in terms of freedom of the press, freedom of worship, freedom of assembly, and freedom of opportunity. Almost every American will agree with that. But it also means freedom from want, freedom from war, freedom from ignorance, and freedom from oppression. The way of the cross in the world—in political, social, and economic terms—means to liberate people from the prisons of class, race, wealth, ideology, and anything else that keeps people down.

Just as Jesus was nailed to the cross for setting people free, those who claim to be his followers will go the way of the cross in setting people free from suffering and degradation, from poverty and hunger, from ignorance and superstition.

All of these ideas flow from Luther's theology of the cross. Luther carried this theology to his death bed. His friends asked him if he was prepared to die in the faith he had preached. Throughout his career Luther had said, "Preach one thing: the wisdom of the cross." Now on his deathbed Luther answered, "Yes. We are beggars. That is true."

It is to be hoped that churches today will learn from Paul's theology of the cross how to be faithful witnesses to Jesus Christ and him crucified;

that they might teach nothing but a theology of the cross;
that they might preach nothing but the crucified God;
that they might trust, not in themselves, but solely in the benefits of the cross;
and that their mission will take shape in the form of the cross of Christ. Amen!

16

By Grace Through Faith in Christ

Romans 1:16-17:

> For I am not ashamed of the gospel; it is the power of God for salvation to everyone who has faith, to the Jew first and also to the Greek. For in it the righteousness of God is revealed through faith for faith; as it is written, "The one who is righteous will live by faith."

The gospel of God in Jesus Christ is the gift of salvation to everyone who believes. That is the heart of the biblical message, and it is also the summary of Martin Luther's theology—we are saved by the grace of God through faith in Jesus Christ who bestows on us the righteousness that God requires and everlasting fellowship with him through the forgiveness of sins. This is the theme of Paul's Letter to the Romans that we will explicate in this brief sermon.

The Gift of Salvation

God created each one of us to live in perfect fellowship with him, to love God and our neighbors as ourselves. However, instead of living our lives in the fullness of love, we act as slaves of sin, guilty before God, hounded by Satan, victims of fear, and destined to die! As individuals we are subject to the vicious cycle of sin, death, and the power of Satan. The gospel declares that God in Christ took it upon himself to break the vicious cycle of slavery, guilt, and fear. The gospel overcomes our estrangement from God, our alienation from our fellow human beings, and our rejection of ourselves.

The gospel means "good news," the good news that while we were dead in our trespasses and sins, enemies of God, slaves of Satan, and damned to hell, God intervened on our behalf to change the conditions under which we exist. God has made us new creatures, perfect and holy in his sight, clothed with the righteousness that Christ gained for us through his sufferings and death on the cross. So we are reconciled to God now and forever. That is the gospel truth. If you believe that, you believe all that really matters in the final analysis—no matter what other problems you may have in your job, in your relationships with other people, or even with yourself. We all struggle to better ourselves, to improve our lot in life, and to make a secure future for our family—but we often fail and find ourselves overcome with a sense of futility. Just at this point we need to have someone who speaks with the authority of God to say to us, "Your sins are forgiven; you are reconciled with God. He loves you and adopts you into his family—no matter what! Not even death can separate you from the love of God."

A huge chasm, a grand canyon, has opened up between the absolute holiness of God and the abysmal sinfulness of the whole human race. People like to sit around and philosophize about what is wrong with the world and what ails the human condition. The Bible says that there is nothing we can do to fix what is wrong—not by means of higher education, better genes, more sophisticated science and technology, or the right kind of politics and economics. Nothing we can do from our side will set things right in a fundamental sense, because we have a God-problem. We are at odds with God. We cannot make things right with God, not with our psychological therapies and self-help techniques, nor with our social projects to make this a better world. The Bible makes clear that the basic issue is not how we feel about ourselves, but how to become right with God. Are we in a right relationship with God now? Do we live with a clear conscience? If we feel that everything is going well with our career, our family, our self-esteem, but if we are not right with God in the depths of our being, then—no matter how many smiles we put on our face—we are at bottom miserable and wretched individuals. "For what will it profit them to gain the whole world and forfeit their life?" (Mark 8:36).

We are saved by grace through faith in Christ Jesus our Lord. This is the Christian message in a nutshell. We are saved by grace alone, not by our own reason and strength. We are saved through faith alone, not by doing good works required by the law. We are saved on account of Christ alone, not by loyalty to any other master.

Congregations love to sing the hymn "Amazing Grace." Why? And why do they sing it with such great gusto? It is because they know intuitively that "there but for the grace of God go I." They sense that everything we have that is true, beautiful, and good comes from grace alone, and that we do not merit a dime's worth of blessings. We could not even believe in the Lord Jesus Christ, except for the wonderful gift of faith.

We did not choose to become believers in Christ; we were chosen; we were elected. Paul goes even further and says that we were "predestined"—a tough notion fraught with much controversy and little understanding. Jesus said to his disciples, "You did not choose me, but I chose you" (John 15:16). Paul said, "For by grace you have been saved through faith, and this is not your own doing; it is the gift of God—not the result of works, so that no one may boast" (Ephesians 2:8-9).

We often hear it said, "There ain't no free lunch." "You get what you pay for." "Everything is tit for tat." "An eye for an eye and a tooth for a tooth." That is the *quid pro quo* philosophy of life. It seems to be the law of life. You can't pick up what you don't lay down. But the good news of the gospel is that God does not deal with us according to the principle of justice, assigning the punishments we rightly deserve for our sins and failures. If God were to throw the full weight of the law against us, we would not stand a chance.

When we think of the grace of God, certain synonyms come to mind —love, kindness, goodness, mercy, favor, goodwill, and generosity. Such is God's attitude toward us poor sinners on account of Christ. God does not love us because we are so lovable. God does not show mercy on us because we are so worthy.

"But God proves his love for us in that while we were still sinners Christ died for us" (Romans 5:8). God did not love us in response to our love for him. God's love is not a reciprocating love. We jilted him. We stood him up. We went in pursuit of other lovers, idols, values, and loyalties. We have not loved God with all our hearts, with all our minds, and with all the powers of our souls. In our natural selves we have been dead to God and alive to the passions of our flesh.

How can we be saved in such a predicament? How can we put God first in our lives, when we love ourselves above all things? When we experience estrangement from someone we love, of course we want to be reconciled, but usually on our own terms. So it is in our relationship with God; we seek reconciliation with God on our terms.

Think of the story of the Tower of Babel, how people wanted to build a tower that would reach to heaven. They did not wish to be surprised by a God who comes to them out of his own freedom—when and where it pleases him. They wanted to be in control—to build a tower that is a work of their own heads and hearts.

Ladders to Heaven

There are basically three ways that people have tried to get to heaven, three ladders people use to climb to God—in short, three ways of salvation that lead upwards to the heavenly city where God dwells in eternal glory.

The first ladder is the way of the intellect, the pursuit of knowledge, using one's mind to fathom the secrets of the universe. Along this path people trust in their own philosophies, make up their own ideologies, and invent their own fabulous myths and systems of doctrine. They are trying to reach ultimate truth through the works of the intellect.

The second ladder to heaven is the way of morality—the pursuit of good works. The moralist lives by the rules, does his duty, and asks to be judged on his performance. God is viewed as an accountant, keeping track of the debits and credits. Jesus is seen as a second Moses, inspiring us to keep the law, both the letter and the spirit of the law.

The third ladder is the way of feeling and emotions. The emotionalist believes that the important thing is to have deep religious experiences, to feel the presence of God, and to feel the excitement of exploring one's inner self. Religion is regarded as a matter of mystical experience, searching for God in the depths of one's soul.

If we could get to God through our intellect, if we could get to God through moral striving, if we could get to God through our feelings, we would not need Christ. Jesus would have lived and died in vain. If we could climb the ladders, God would not have had to descend to our earthly level in the person of his incarnate Son Jesus Christ. If we could storm the gates of heaven by exercising our intellects, wills, or feelings, Christ would not have had to appear on earth in human likeness, taking the lowly form of a servant, becoming obedient to the point of death—even death on a cross.

Paul and Silas were sitting in jail praying and singing hymns to God while the other prisoners were listening to them. Suddenly there was an earthquake, shaking the foundations of the prison. Immediately all the doors sprang open, and everyone's chains were unfastened. When the jailer woke up and saw the prison doors wide open, he drew his sword and was about to kill himself, as he assumed that all the prisoners had escaped. Paul shouted in a loud voice. "Do not harm yourself, for we are all here" (Acts 16:28). Then the jailer called for lights, and he rushed in and fell down trembling before Paul and Silas. The jailer cried out to Paul and Silas, "Sirs, what must I do to be saved?" (Acts 16:30b). Paul and Silas answered him, "Believe on the Lord Jesus, and you will be saved" (Acts 16:31). They did not say, "Think positively about yourself; trust in your own possibilities; get in touch with your feelings; find something good to do with yourself, and you will gain higher self-esteem." They simply said, "Believe in the Lord Jesus and you will be saved." Is not that too easy and cheap, to place your entire hope for salvation on someone else, on Jesus Christ? There must be something that we must do to be saved. And why Christ? Why is Christ necessary for salvation?

The answer is that Jesus, as he is portrayed in the New Testament, is the one who fulfilled the law. He is the one who subdued the wrath of God by taking our sins to the cross. Jesus is the one who struggled against Satan and conquered. He is the one who triumphed over death through his resurrection from the grave. Jesus accomplished all these things which no one else has done or could do, and he did it for our sakes, so that we might be reconciled to God and enter into his kingdom now and forever.

The Good Work of Faith

Believe in the Lord Jesus, and you will be saved. Is not the act of believing at least something we must do by our own free will? Is not faith a good work that each one of us must do? Do we not then contribute something to our own salvation, after all? Theologians have fought over this issue for generations. Some say that faith is something we are able to accomplish by our own free will. They believe that since human beings are born with free will, they must be free to accept or reject God's offer of salvation and to do good works that merit salvation. This was the teaching of Pelagius, a British monk who lived in the fifth century. His teaching was condemned as a heresy by several councils of the church. Others teach (Lutherans among them) that we humans have lost our freedom in relation to the things of God, that our wills are in bondage ever since the fall of Adam and Eve. We are free in mundane matters, such as what time to get up, what church to attend, whom to marry, how many children to have, or what profession to seek. But in relation to God we are not free. This was the teaching of Augustine in the fifth century, a fierce opponent of Pelagius.

Martin Luther, himself a good Augustinian monk, taught that we humans are slaves to sin, in bondage to Satan, and under a death sentence. Only the grace of God is the power to make us free. For freedom Christ has set us free, so we are free by the grace of God, not of ourselves, lest we should boast. Even our faith is the work of the Holy Spirit, a sheer gift. Luther said in his explanation to the third article of the Apostles' Creed: "I believe that I cannot by my own reason or strength believe in the Lord Jesus Christ. But the Holy Spirit has called me through the gospel, enlightened me with his gifts, and sanctified and preserved me in the truth faith."

Of course, when I believe in Jesus Christ, my believing is something that I do. But the very fact that I am able to repent and believe is the work of the Holy Spirit through the power of the Word. The grace of God creates the freedom of faith and makes me an adopted child of his beloved family—all through no merit or worthiness on my part.

Faith is a good work, to be sure, but it is a good work of the Spirit of God. We are saved by faith alone, solely on account of Christ. If our wills are in bondage, how then can we choose to believe in Christ? We can do so because the Spirit of God is powerful enough to deliver us from this bondage.

So we have no need of ladders to climb to heaven, no need to build a Tower of Babel. We are liberated from the business of having to save ourselves. When we stand before God in the clear light of the gospel, we have nothing of which to boast. All is of grace and that is our joy. Because we are free, we are slaves of Christ. We can offer all our faculties—our minds and ideas, our wills and moral strivings, our feelings and emotions—to the service of God and our fellow human beings. We do not do all these things in order to get saved. We do all such things because we have received the free gift of salvation through Christ our Lord in the power of the Holy Spirit. Amen!

17

The Happy Exchange

Luke 16: 19-31:

There was a rich man who was dressed in purple and fine linen and who feasted sumptuously every day. And at his gate lay a poor man named Lazarus, covered with sores, who longed to satisfy his hunger with what fell from the rich man's table; even the dogs would come and lick his sores. The poor man died and was carried away by the angels to be with Abraham. The rich man also died and was buried. In Hades, where he was being tormented, he looked up and saw Abraham far away with Lazarus by his side. He called out, "Father Abraham, have mercy on me, and send Lazarus to dip the tip of his finger in water and cool my tongue; for I am in agony in these flames." But Abraham said, "Child, remember that during your lifetime you received your good things, and Lazarus in like manner evil things; but now he is comforted here, and you are in agony. Besides all this, between you and us a great chasm has been fixed, so that those who might want to pass from here to you cannot do so, and no one can cross from there to us." He said, "Then, father, I beg you to send him to my father's house—for I have five brothers—that he may warn them, so that they will not also come into this place of torment." Abraham replied, "They have Moses and the prophets; they should listen to them." He said, "No, father Abraham; but if someone goes to them from the dead, they will repent." He said to him, "If they do not listen to Moses and the prophets, neither will they be convinced even if someone rises from the dead."

The Gap Between Rich and Poor

The modern world has found no solution to the problem of the widening gap between the rich and the poor. Most of the six billion people in the world are desperately poor; some of us are rich. Luke records that Jesus told this story about the rich man—let us call him Dives—and the poor man Lazarus. Apparently the gap between the rich and the poor was characteristic of the ancient world as well. The Bible frequently makes reference to this phenomenon. Jesus reserved some of his harshest words for the rich. "But woe to you who are rich, for you have received your consolation" (Luke 6:24). "Truly I tell you, it will be hard for a rich person to enter the kingdom of heaven. Again, I tell you, it is easier for a camel to go through the eye of a needle than someone who is rich to enter the kingdom of God" (Matthew 19:23-24).

Down through the centuries words like these have provided a convenient occasion to bash the rich. That is the poor man's revenge. In the refrain of one spiritual: "You can have the world, but we'll take Jesus." The rich will get their just reward, cast into outer darkness, "weeping and gnashing of teeth" (Matthew 8:12). But what strange tricks people play on themselves. When the poor become rich, do they behave any differently? In Jesus' day the Pharisees believed that being rich was a sign of God's blessing. So did the Puritans. If you are rich, you must be doing something right and God must be pleased with you. But if you are poor, it's because you are a no good lazy bum and you are getting what you deserve.

There is a great mystery about the inequality between the rich and the poor. The sharpest minds have tried to figure out how to narrow the gap. The chief attraction of the teachings of Karl Marx among poor people and poor nations is the promise of communism to get rid of the gap between the classes and to give everyone an equal share of paradise on earth. Jesus postponed the punishment of the rich until the next life; Marx wanted to bring down the guillotine of judgment against the rich in this life. Wherever communism has spread, the heads of the rich have been the first to roll off the butcher's block.

We could go on in this vein and try to glean some moral philosophy or economic wisdom out of this parable of the rich man and the poor man. We could indulge in endless moralization, as many sermons have done, about how it is okay to be rich, if only we have the right attitude toward the poor and give to charity. We may be only quibbling about how many crumbs we will give to the beggars. Or we can rationalize that it is okay to accumulate a lot of possessions, so long as we are not possessed by them. Or, perhaps, it does not matter whether one is rich or poor, if one's heart is in the right place.

This parable is neither a slap in the face of the rich nor a cheap consolation for the poor. It does not teach that the rich will go to hell because they are rich, nor that the poor will get to heaven because they are poor. It certainly does not teach that God prefers people to be poor and that he hates the rich. After all, Abraham himself was a rich man. This parable does not teach anything about God's preferential option for the poor, to use the current jargon of liberation theology. This parable does not teach that poor people are virtuous or that poverty is a condition that we should embrace and celebrate. In fact, poverty can be quite ugly; there is nothing glamorous about it. We should not turn Lazarus into a saint worthy of entering the gate of heaven.

If you have ever been poor, if you have been in the same predicament as poor Tevye in *Fiddler on the Roof*, you too would want to sing:

> If I were a rich man . . . all day long I'd build a big, tall house with rooms by the dozen, right in the middle of the town, a fine tin roof and real wooden floors below. There would be one long staircase just going up, and one even longer coming down, and one more leading nowhere just for show.

That is the eloquent cry of a poor man who dreams of a better life. But that is not what this parable is about either. Nor do we find in it the elements of a Christian economics. Christianity does not have a solution to the gap between the rich and the poor. Albert Schweitzer read this parable and thought it meant that he should go to Africa as a medical missionary; he saw Africa as the poor beggar sitting at the gate of Europe. He left the academic halls of Europe where he had earned five Ph.D.s and went to care for his poor brothers and sisters in Lambarene. So it was also with St. Francis and Mother Teresa; they answered a call to enter the world of beggars to bring hope and dignity to their wretched state.

The Reversal of Roles

Now we are getting closer to the meaning of this parable, but we still need to go farther. Before we take this parable as a story about our life, troubled as we are about the gap between the rich and the poor, we should let it take us into the wider and deeper drama of the whole biblical story of God and the salvation of humankind. This story about Dives the rich man and Lazarus the poor man hinges on their dramatic switching of roles, their exchange of places. Not only here but throughout Jesus' teachings, he placed the whole of human life under the spotlight of eternity, revealing the paradox at the heart of the gospel. All the signs are reversed in the kingdom of God. The last will be first and the first will be last. Sinners, not the righteous, will be the first to enter the kingdom of God. Whoever would be the greatest among you must be the servant of all. This is the topsy-turvy world of God's kingdom in which the roles are reversed. The rich will be lost and the poor will be saved.

What on earth can this principle of reversal mean? It puts an end to all human calculations; it introduces us into the new math of the kingdom of God. Plus is minus and minus is plus, turning things around at the bottom line. It all began in heaven, in the eternal counsel of God, with the decision of the Father to send his only Son into the world in the form of a beggar to take our place, to make us rich.

> Let the same mind be in you that was in Christ Jesus, who, though he was in the form of God, did not regard equality with God as something to be exploited, but emptied himself, taking the form of a slave, being born in human likeness. And being found in human form, he humbled himself and became obedient to the point of death—even death on a cross" (Philippians 2:5-8).

The good news of the incarnation of the Son of God is that he exchanged places with us. The rich and the poor have exchanged places. The eternal glory of God has been exchanged for the rags of a beggar Christ, in whom there is "no form or comeliness" (Isaiah 53:2). Normally when we think of God, we think of power, omnipotence, eternal glory, infinite wisdom, and heavenly majesty. We would expect God to identify with the clout of the rich man, someone who is in charge of things. But that is not the way in the kingdom of God. For God meets us in the form of total contrast, in the helpless and humiliated figure of the dying man on the cross.

Martin Luther used the image of a scale. When God throws himself on the scale as a poor man in the person of the suffering and dying Jesus, then his side goes down, and our side goes up and we become rich. He became poor for us, going all the way down to hell, so that we might become rich, ascending all the way to heaven. God suffered, God bled, and God died, so that poor sinners might be made alive and join the company of saints for all eternity. This is the dramatic reversal of roles we see in the gospel story.

Only in the gospel do we find this paradoxical truth that God would hang on the gallows so that we might be lifted up. Luther called this turn of events the "happy exchange." He said, "Lord Jesus, you are my righteousness, just as I am your sin. You have taken upon yourself what you were not and you have given to me what I was not." The man from heaven has descended into hell so that we might all rise and ascend to be with God in heaven. That is almost too good to be true, but that is the deep mystery hidden in the parable of Dives and Lazarus, cast against the backdrop of eternity. God in Christ takes upon himself all our horrible sins, so that we might be clothed in the robes of his righteousness.

If we do not see the deeper mystery of the gospel in this parable, we might as well sit down and talk about economics, and debate the contrasting views of Adam Smith and Karl Marx. But this parable is not about economics; it offers no solution to the problem of the gap between the rich and the poor. It is about eternal life. The poor man's name is Lazarus; that name means "help in God." Lazarus has come to the gate empty-handed. Now he must cast himself upon the mercy of another. The poor beggar cannot help himself.

Then, Who Can Be Saved?

The truth is, we are like Lazarus in desperate need of the help of God. The rich man lived with the illusion that he was the "master of his fate and the captain of his soul." He believed he could buy his way, that money could secure his life. Are we also too preoccupied with accumulating more wealth, enjoying more expensive toys, name-brand clothes, exotic vacations, and beautiful bodies? We may not be as rich as Malcolm Forbes, but our hearts beat to the same tune, with eyes trained to leap to the bottom line, counting our stocks and bonds, money market funds, pension plans, and anything that will make us rich and secure our future. But what good does that do, if we should win the lottery and allow it to consume our souls? That is the plight of the rich man. He believed he was the lord of his life. He had money, power, and status; he had lost interest in the tender qualities of compassion and mercy, the helping hand, the open heart, patience, humility, and friendship.

Friedrich Nietzsche was the nineteenth century architect of Adolf Hitler's philosophy of the master race. Although he was born and raised in a Protestant parsonage, Nietzsche came to despise Christianity. He railed against the beggar image of Christ, because Christ taught the self-belittling qualities of a poor Lazarus. Instead, Nietzsche glorified the virtues of the master race, of the superman with his power, pride, and control. That is the spirit of Dives the rich man. It leads to death and destruction. Yet, we are seduced into believing that the way of the rich man guarantees the good life, happiness, and a secure future.

George Orwell, author of *Animal Farm* and *1984*, tells of a cruel joke he played on a wasp. The wasp was sucking jam on his plate, so Mr. Orwell cut it in half. The wasp paid no attention, merely went on with his meal, while a thin stream of jam trickled out of his severed esophagus. Only when he tried to fly away did the wasp grasp the dreadful thing that had happened to him.

So it was with the rich man. Only when it was too late did he realize what a dreadful thing had happened to him. How can we avoid such a fate? How can we who are the brothers and sisters of Dives wake up to realize what is happening before it is too late? We are not only talking about one rich man, but about a rich people, a rich nation, even a rich church. The spirit of Dives invades our lives not only as private individuals but permeates everything we are a part of, our families, clubs, organizations, and even our church. How can we avoid this fate before it is too late? Some churches wish to be great and glorious in worldly terms. Some church leaders wish to be vocal and victorious in political terms. So again the question, how can we avoid this fate before it is too late? Father Abraham says, "You have the law and the prophets."

We have a long and illustrious tradition, a reforming tradition with many heroes of the faith, an evangelical tradition with a strong theology of the cross, a catholic tradition with a full liturgical life, an apostolic tradition that has sent missionaries throughout the world, and an ecumenical tradition that works for the unity of Christ's church on earth. All of these traditions make us very rich. So we must ask ourselves, what are we doing with our riches? Where are we going?

We can avoid the fate of the rich man before it is too late. We have the Scriptures to guide us. They witness to "the way, the truth, and the life." They convey the gospel that Christ died for our sins and was raised for our redemption. That is the core of our faith and the only hope of our salvation.

My favorite motto for my own life and my calling as a theologian of the church is one that I found at the end of a book entitled *Christianity and History*, authored by the British historian, Herbert Butterfield. These are the words: "Stick to Jesus Christ, and as for all the rest be totally uncommitted." May that also be deeply etched into our purpose and mission as a church in the years to come. Amen!

The Vertical and Horizontal Dimensions of Forgiveness

Matthew 18:21-22:

> Then Peter came and said to him, "Lord, if another member of the church sins against me, how often should I forgive? As many as seven times?" Jesus said to him, "Not seven times, but, I tell you, seventy-seven times."

Ephesians 1:7-8a:

> In him (Christ) we have redemption through his blood, the forgiveness of our trespasses, according to the riches of his grace that he lavished on us.

At an anniversary we generally focus on such things as memory and identity—remembering who we are as a people—and on gratitude and vision—thanking God for the promise of the future. At the heart of all of this is the forgiveness of sins. Each one of us became a believer in Christ and a member of his church through our baptism for the remission of sins. As we confess our sins, we receive absolution from our pastor—the declaration of the entire forgiveness of all our sins. As we eat the bread and drink the wine, we share in the new covenant in the blood of Jesus, shed for us and all people for the forgiveness of sin.

No Room for Forgiveness

The book of Genesis has a happy ending. Joseph's brothers had sold him into slavery. They had been jealous of him because he was their father's favorite son. This little Israeli boy meanwhile became the minister of agriculture in Pharaoh's Egypt, a very powerful and successful ruler.

Many years later the brothers came to Joseph to beg for forgiveness. Joseph had the opportunity to get back at them, to make them pay for their crime, but he simply forgave them. He knew in his heart that it was God's way, and the only way to turn something evil into something good. We live in a society in which forgiveness is becoming ever rarer. As I approached an intersection with my car, a pedestrian taunted me, daring me to hit him, yelling, "Hit me, I want to get rich." One little pop, and people are looking for a lawyer, trying to get even, bilking the system of justice for the last drop of vengeance. The lack of forgiveness is a fact of modern life. There is a real shortage of forgiveness, and an excess of hatred and violence.

Remember how President Bush in his inaugural address appealed for a "kinder and gentler nation" and how in the years since, to the contrary, we have plunged into the vicious cycle of revenge and retaliation— becoming a nation of people at war among ourselves. We say we are looking for justice, and, without doubt, when certain minorities are being deprived basic justice, we must fight for their rights and demand justice.

But justice is not enough. Justice without the spirit of forgiveness cannot produce a kinder and gentler nation. Government, legislation, a police force, law courts, and jails can deter us from doing bad things, but they cannot make people love each other. Apart from the loving spirit of forgiveness, we are stuck with the law of nature, the logic of vengeance, the spirit of retaliation, the kind of justice that demands an "eye for an eye, and a tooth for a tooth." Fear, hate, enmity, and jealousy —such emotions are deeply embedded in our human nature. We cannot change the mechanism that creates the expanding spiral of violence in our society today.

Many worldly-wise people make fun of forgiveness. They do not believe it makes sense. They ridicule the need for forgiveness; the forgiving attitude is supposedly a mark of weakness, a sign that a person is lacking self-confidence. Friedrich Nietzsche and Sigmund Freud regarded the whole idea of forgiveness as unacceptable, especially Jesus' command to love our enemies. Nietzsche believed that forgiveness makes one a beggar. Qualities such as sympathy, mercy, compassion, humility, and friendliness are for softies, diminishing the human spirit. Instead, Nietzsche said, we should promote the qualities of the superman, the self-glorifying virtues of the master race that Adolf Hitler tried to produce—qualities of pride, power, superiority, and domination. There is no room for forgiveness in Nietzsche's paradigm of what it takes to be a superior human being and a good society.

The Leaven of Forgiveness

Forgiveness is the only way to a kinder and gentler nation. Without the leaven of forgiveness, the social bonds of living in community become hard and inflexible. The nation's statistics on suicide and divorce continue to rise, families become dysfunctional, children rise up against their parents as pay-back for years of abuse. At the most primitive level and at the first instance the human inclination is not to ask forgiveness but to get revenge. "I want to get even" is the prevailing sentiment.

The fact is forgiveness is a revolutionary reality. It is not doing what comes naturally. Only a person who has experienced forgiveness is able to forgive. That explains why the landlord in the text we read is so hard on his servant. The servant had received forgiveness from his landlord; he was expected to do likewise. But he didn't. Forgiveness is the logic of the new world order created by Jesus through his sacrifice on the cross. Because the servant refused to forgive as he had been forgiven, he excluded himself from the kingdom of God.

God has broken the spiral of vengeance, violence, and retaliation by sending his only Son Jesus into the world to engage the powers and principalities of this age. Jesus exhibited and embodied God's way of mercy, forgiveness, and unconditional love. He said to Peter that he is to forgive "not seven times, but, I tell you, seventy times seven" (Matthew 18:22). And then on the cross Jesus did as much when he cried out, "Father, forgive them"—namely, the priests, scribes, Pharisees, politicians, soldiers, and all who had a hand in accusing, condemning, and nailing this innocent man to a cross. Forgiveness was in the heart of Jesus; he did not condemn sinners nor did he condone their sins. Jesus did not say that sin does not matter. He did not teach that all actions are morally relative. Sinners are real sinners, and their sins are real sins. By his death on the cross, Jesus showed that he took sin seriously. He paid the full price by giving up his life so that love might break the vicious cycle of sin, vengeance, and violence. Sin and forgiveness go together like hand in glove.

The reason many people think they have no need of forgiveness is because they have no sense of sin. Dr. Karl Menninger, a famous Christian psychiatrist, wrote a book with the title, *Whatever Happened to Sin?* In it he laments that the concept of sin has fallen out of modern psychology and psychotherapy. Where there is no awareness of sin, there is no felt need for forgiveness, and where there is no need for forgiveness, there is no need for Christ and his sacrificial death on the cross.

Not only is sin missing from modern psychotherapy and medical science, it has fallen flat in the modern church and popular preaching. Sin does not fit the religion of "positive thinking" and the "be-happy attitudes." Sin is too negative; it makes people feel like there is something fundamentally wrong with them deep down in their souls. H. Richard Niebuhr, formerly professor of theology at Yale Divinity School, characterized the preaching of liberal Protestantism this way: "A God without wrath brought people without sin into a kingdom without judgment through the ministry of Christ without the cross." No wrath, no sin, no judgment, no cross—ergo, no need for Christ! That is the predicament of religion in America without the gospel. It may be popular; it may be successful; it may be entertaining, calculated to make the church grow. We need to ask ourselves, however, are we forgetting that the church is in the business of forgiveness, that its mission is to preach the gospel of forgiveness in Jesus' name to set people free from bondage to sin and the penalty of eternal death?

A boy was with his dad visiting a great cathedral. As they walked under the giant arches, the boy asked, "Dad, what is the big plus sign up front?" "Why, that's the cross on the high altar. But son, you're exactly right, that's what the cross is, God's eternal plus sign, which adds something new to our life." That something new is the forgiveness of sins—the gateway to sanctification and the pursuit of holy living. There can be no new life and freedom, no friendship with God and hope of eternal salvation, and no membership in the communion of saints without the forgiveness of sins.

Why is the forgiveness of sins so absolutely essential? Look at this way. In Wisconsin we had a cottage at the lake. When we planned to stay for a month, we knew we would have a problem with the garbage. We began putting the garbage in a few empty milk containers. But soon they filled up and began to pile up. So we went out and bought a garbage can. But eventually that filled up. We got a larger galvanized can, and for a week or so it seemed we had taken care of the problem. But we knew we were only stalling. We had not really solved the problem of garbage disposal. One day our neighbor told us what he did. There is a local garbage collector; he could add us to his route. The point is this: We cannot handle the garbage of sin, guilt, fear, and death by ourselves. We need an outside agency to take the garbage away, the poisonous pollution of sin that breeds spiritual cancer in our bodies and souls.

Jesus died for us and he was raised from the dead for us to deal with our human problem of sin, the sickness unto death. "For while we were still weak, at the right time Christ died for the ungodly" (Romans 5:6). This is truly God's amazing grace.

The Church as the Dispenser of Forgiveness

We cannot receive the forgiveness of sins without someone to declare it to us. If we have sinned, we cannot forgive ourselves. Luther said:

> You cannot sit down in some corner and wait for an angel to come from heaven and announce to you, "Your sins are forgiven." Not any angel, Luther said, but your pastor has been given a special commission from the Lord to say to you, "I, in God's place, announce to you through Christ forgiveness of all your sins"; when this happens, you are to be certain that by such an external word your sins are truly and surely forgiven, for God's Word cannot lie and deceive you. Thank God for his mercy, that he wants to forgive sins in no other way than by giving the power to do it to human beings in the church.

God has elected the church to do some things that no other agency or institution can do—baptize, absolve, preach, and celebrate the Lord's Supper. We cannot get the absolute word of forgiveness in Jesus' name any other place than in the church. That is the special commission that God has given to the church, to be a sanctuary where the forgiveness of sins is freely given for the healing of our broken lives and burdened souls.

In Luther's day there were "spiritualists" who said they did not need the church. They believed they could enjoy a personal relationship with God apart from the church. They supposedly had no need of a minister to mediate the forgiveness of sins. They had no need of such external things as water in baptism, bread and wine in holy communion, or the spoken words of a minister. Supposedly, all that matters is how one feels inside. Luther said "no" to them; it does not work that way. We cannot mend our ruptured relationship with God by a do-it-yourself approach. Our feelings have nothing to do with the reality of the situation. We may be deluded. Luther said that we cannot infer from our feelings that God has forgiven us. The important point is not how we feel about God but how God feels about us. Every Lord's Day we come to church to hear the word of absolution spoken by our pastor in God's name and by his authority, granting us the entire forgiveness of all our sins. Amen!

19

The Reformation in an Ecumenical Age

Romans 3:19-28:

> Now we know that whatever the law says, it speaks to those who are under the law, so that every mouth may be silenced, and the whole world may be held accountable to God. For no human being will be justified in his sight by deeds prescribed by the law, for through the law comes the knowledge of sin.
>
> But now, apart from the law, the righteousness of God has been disclosed, and is attested by the law and the prophets, the righteousness of God through faith in Jesus Christ for all who believe. For there is no distinction, since all have sinned and fall short of the glory of God; they are now justified by his grace as a gift, through the redemption that is in Christ Jesus, whom God put forward as a sacrifice of atonement by his blood, effective through faith. He did this to show his righteousness, because in his divine forbearance he had passed over the sins previously committed; it was to prove at the present time that he himself is righteous and that he justifies the one who has faith in Jesus.

Reformation Day is appointed for October 31, the day Martin Luther nailed his ninety-five theses to the door of the castle church in Wittenberg, Germany. The original point of this day was to give thanks for the spread of the Reformation throughout the world. The heart of the celebration was Martin Luther's reaffirmation of the gospel of Christ according to St. Paul, so clearly spelled out in Paul's letters to the Romans and Galatians.

Luther's Reaffirmation of the Gospel

In his letters to the Romans and the Galatians, Paul taught that a person becomes right with God solely by receiving through faith the gift of God's righteousness in Jesus Christ. The corollary of this proposition is that no human being can be justified in God's sight by doing this, that, or the other thing—no matter how good. The law of God pressures us to do a lot of good things that we feel duty bound to do, but a thousand such good works cannot tip the scale of God's justice in our favor. For we have all sinned and fall short of the glory of God. The deficit, the bondage, the predicament is so great, there is nothing we can do from the human side to set ourselves free, to make things right with God. Christ himself is the cloak of righteousness; it is on account of Christ alone that we gain the hope of salvation.

We have just described what is called the doctrine of justification by faith. This doctrine is so fundamental that for centuries it has been called "the article by which the church stands or falls." The doctrine of justification sits on a tripod, as it were, a three-legged stool consisting of three "onlys"—only by grace, only by faith, and only on account of Christ.

That is the gist of the good news. Now the bad news is that Christians have shed a lot of blood fighting over this doctrine. Lutherans and Catholics have been fighting each other for almost half a millennium. They even got divorced squabbling over the meaning of the doctrine of justification. In the sixteenth century they condemned each other's teachings, and they anathematized each other. They split the church. Lutherans went to the North, Catholics to the South. There are not many Catholics in Norway and Sweden, and not many Lutherans in Spain and Italy. This has been a blood-stained doctrine; it has been used like a sword plunged into the bleeding heart of Christian Europe, setting members of the one body of Christ at war with each other.

Ever since the separation of Catholics and Lutherans, the festival of the Reformation often became the occasion for Lutherans to bash Catholics and to caricature their teachings in self-righteous rhetoric. Lutherans accused Catholics of teaching salvation by good works, by prayers, fasting, and alms-giving, or getting a friend or relative out of purgatory by purchasing a letter of indulgence.

But then a miracle happened, much later. Along came the ecumenical movement, and things began to change. The Second Vatican Council called for the end of inter-religious rivalry and recrimination and for the beginning of ecumenical dialogue. Lutherans and Catholics, both in the United States and internationally, entered into an ongoing series of ecumenical dialogues, taking up disputed doctrines and discussing controversial points of basic difference. How things have changed! Who could have imagined that by the end of the second millennium, Lutherans and Catholics would announce that they have reached a fundamental consensus on the very doctrine—the doctrine of justification by faith—that divided them at the time of the Reformation? Who could have believed that Lutherans and Catholics were moving on converging paths, leading to greater visible unity and the hope of full communion? This is not merely a matter of human planning and bureaucratic achievement. The Holy Spirit of God, the Spirit of peace and reconciliation, is at work to answer the prayer for Christian unity that Jesus prayed at the hour of his passion, "That they may all be one. As you, Father, are in me and I am in you, may they also be in us, so that the world may believe that you have sent me" (John 17:21).

The Spirit of Ecumenism

The Second Vatican Council declared that "people of both sides were to blame." It declared that "all those justified by faith are incorporated into Christ," and that "all those who believe in Christ belong by right to the one church of Christ." The ecumenical spirit of Pope John XXIII and of the Second Vatican Council was contagious. It increased the desire among Christians for a change of heart and growth toward full communion in faithfulness to Christ and the gospel. On the occasion of the pope's visit to the land of Luther in 1980, he said, "Let us no more pass judgment on one another. Let us rather recognize our guilt."

When the ecumenical spirit first spread among pastors and congregations, it put a damper on celebrating the Festival of the Reformation in the same old polemical way. How do we celebrate the Reformation in an ecumenical age when, instead of being nasty and mean-spirited, we are supposed to be nice and tolerant of other Christians? The old way was so much more reassuring. We are right, and they are wrong, period. Once a year we could trot out our familiar fighting slogans, wave our crusading banners, sing our chauvinistic rousers, thanking God that ours is the church that preaches the pure truth of the gospel and the clearest message of salvation.

The spirit of ecumenism has changed all that. For us the meaning of the Reformation is not for us to divide and conquer, to separate Christians and communities from one another. The biblical doctrine of justification by faith is a truth that belongs to all Christians and the whole Christian church on earth. The point of the Reformation was not to start a new kind of Christianity, but to reform and renew the church from the top down by means of the gospel, according to the Scriptures. That is what the word "evangelical" means—doing things according to the gospel. We as a people of the Reformation are ecumenically committed, or else we are simply traitors. People who share the Lutheran heritage are committed to the ecumenical movement promoting Christian unity as an organic part of our faith and mission, pervading all that we are and do.

Luther had no intention of starting a new church, a new sect or cult. Luther said:

> I ask that people make no reference to my name; let them call themselves Christians, not Lutherans. Who is Luther, after all? The teaching is not mine; nor was I crucified for anyone. . . . No, my dear friends, let us abolish all party names and call ourselves Christians, after Christ whose teaching we hold.

Ecumenism fosters not only a dialogue of love but also a dialogue of truth. It is the truth, and only the truth, that makes us free. We cannot have ecumenical dialogue leading to Christian unity and full communion between divided churches based on falsehoods, sentimentality, or the pretense of agreement. "If you continue in my word, you are truly my disciples," said Jesus, "and you will know the truth, and the truth will make you free" (John 8:32). Ecumenism based on the gospel truth does not simply mean being tolerant and nice to each other. Love for the truth drives us to be reunited with our fellow Christians, to overcome our separations in the name of Christ who is "the way, the truth, and the life." No longer do we see other Christians as enemies or strangers. We see them as brothers and sisters whom God loves and for whose salvation Jesus died and was raised from the dead.

The Joint Declaration on the Doctrine of Justification

Lutherans around the world have agreed to bury the hatchet on the doctrine of justification. The Roman Catholic Church at its highest level of authority has also agreed to cancel the mutual condemnations of the Reformation era. This means that God is repossessing his disobedient and fragmented church, a church that created the scandal of disunity and division and that merited the scorn and derision of unbelievers. Unbelieving scoffers could exclaim, "Look at the Christians! How they fight and hate each other, in the name of Christ." Now things are changing at an incredible pace. The joint Lutheran–Catholic common declaration on justification means that a consensus is building and the old condemnations are fading away. Because justification is a central article of faith, it will lead to further ecumenical conversation and cooperation, moving the churches toward unity and communion. Those who are reconciled with God in Christ must become reconciled with each other. That is the ecumenical imperative.

There is no better way to celebrate the festival of the Reformation than for Lutherans and Catholics to do it together, and to welcome other Christians and churches to join them. Lutherans have adopted a document that confesses the basic truth on which the Reformation took its stand. Luther at the Diet of Worms cried, "Here I stand. I can do no other. So help me God!" That is a Promethean outcry of a single individual. Now we can confess jointly as communities, Lutherans and Catholics together, a whole series of things.

According to the "Joint Declaration on the Doctrine of Justification," Lutherans and Catholics confess: 1) that all persons depend completely on the saving grace of God for their salvation; 2) that God forgives sin by grace and at the same time frees human beings from sin's enslaving power and imparts the gift of new life in Christ; 3) that sinners are justified by faith in the saving action of God in Christ; 4) that in baptism the Holy Spirit unites one with Christ, justifies, and truly renews the person; 5) that persons are justified by faith in the gospel "apart from works prescribed by the law"; 6) that the faithful can rely on the mercy and promises of God; 7) that good works follow justification and are its fruits.

Then the Joint Declaration states that "a consensus in basic truths of the doctrine of justification now exists between Lutherans and Catholics." It goes on to declare that the mutual condemnations of the sixteenth century no longer apply to the teachings of the other church. It concludes with this prayer: "We give thanks to the Lord for this decisive step forward on the way to overcoming the division of the church. We ask the Holy Spirit to lead us further toward that visible unity which is Christ's will."

Remaining Obstacles to Church Unity

That is truly remarkable, without a doubt a miracle of grace! Nothing of its kind has occurred in the last five hundred years. This does not mean that Lutherans and Catholics can yet celebrate Holy

Communion at the same altar. I should qualify that statement. Most Lutherans are willing and perhaps most Catholics are also willing, but they have not received permission from the Vatican. Yet, together we have come a long way. A few decades ago we could not have imagined it. The doctrine of justification by grace through faith in Christ alone is now acceptable teaching in the Roman Catholic Church. That is finally all that Luther asked for. He did not ask for everyone to agree with him on everything, only that he would have the freedom to preach the gospel according to the Scriptures. Now that is possible. No one would be excommunicated in the Roman Catholic Church today for believing, teaching, and confessing what the Lutherans at Augsburg did in the sixteenth century. But we still have a long way to go. We cannot rest on our oars and drift downstream.

The world around us does not want the unity of the church for which Christ prayed, because the disunity of the churches is deeply connected to the world's unbelief. As long as the churches are divided, the world feels exonerated from having to believe in the truth of Christ, who is the head of the body, the church. If the members are warring against each other, that reflects badly on the head of the household, the one in charge. The lack of Christian unity is linked to the apostasy of the millions of baptized Christians in the West, who no longer believe and no longer participate in the life of the church, its Sunday worship services, and its sacramental celebrations. There is a reason for that, and the reason is us, our unbelief, our disunity, and the scandal of our divisions.

The question remains: How can the unity for which Christ prayed be restored to a divided church? How much farther must we travel until the full unity of the church will be attained and we can all celebrate at the one table of the Lord? For a thousand years the church was united, East and West. Then the Great Schism occurred in 1054 A.D. In the sixteenth century the church in the West became split down the middle. How can unity be restored in this third millennium? That is the challenge that lies before all of us. That is what God calls us to do, to become visibly and manifestly, obediently and faithfully the one, holy, catholic, and apostolic church so that the world might believe. This is God's will for Christ's church.

One final caveat: There is no down side to this proposition. Christian unity is not a zero sum game. There are no losers, only winners. In the reunited church of the future, we will not be asked to lose our identity. There will be no mega-church unification in thrall to a single centralized ecclesiastical bureaucracy, located in Geneva, New York, or Rome. This is what the fear-mongers are telling us. It is not true. Lutherans will continue to be Lutheran—holding on to justification by faith, perhaps mixed with lutefisk and lefse. Reformed will do no better than to remain true to their Calvinist moorings, Methodists will be free to be Wesleyan, and the Eastern Orthodox, Greek or Russian, will not become westernized Roman Christians. Christians in Asia, Africa, and Latin American are showing us new ways of worshiping Christ and expressing Christian truth. The bottom line is that we may all be one in Christ, all members of his one body, representing a magnificent plurality of languages, races, cultures, nationalities, and a great symphony of Christian traditions, with different ways of worship, prayer, and witness—which, after all, is what it means to be catholic with a small "c."

The ecumenical train will move on inexorably, with or without us, if it is God's will, and we believe it is. It is the answer to Jesus' prayer in John 17: "That all may be one, so that the world might believe." The truth of justification for which the Reformation stands has now been affirmed by the Roman Catholic Church in its essentials. Some critics say that differences remain, and that is true. However, similar differences exist between various Lutheran traditions and theologians. The common declaration on justification says we are united in the truth of the gospel. That is a lot for which to be grateful. But we still have to find a way to apply that truth in matters that continue to keep us strangers from one another's altars, pulpits, and pews. That is the work of decades to come. Finally, it is God's work. We are invited to be a part of it, pastors, lay folks, and theologians. It is a great and wonderful thing to be able to leave behind our divisions in order to seek to re-establish the unity that God wills for his church. Amen!

PART FIVE

Ministry and Sacraments

The ministry of the church in history and today is modeled on the ministry that Jesus gave to his apostles. The simplest New Testament expression for this transaction is Jesus' saying to his disciples: "He who hears you hears me" (Luke 10:16). The chief concern of ministers is that the true voice of the gospel be heard, because whoever hears the gospel the apostles preached hears Christ himself.

The early church confronted this question: How can the community of believers in Jesus remain apostolic after all the apostles have died? Initially the church received its identity from the living witness of the apostles to Jesus of Nazareth, his life, death, and resurrection. Where this witness was absent, there could be no faith in Jesus and no community could assemble for worship in his name. The church was built on the foundation of the apostolic witness to Jesus: "For no one can lay any foundation other than the one that has been laid; that foundation is Jesus Christ (1 Corinthians 3:11).

The early church had to improvise structures of ministry to keep the church apostolic in post-apostolic times. Through prayer and the laying on of hands, the apostles passed on their authority to those they chose to hold offices of leadership. They were called presbyters and bishops. After decades of ecumenical dialogue, churches still lack consensus on the method of apostolic succession. Despite this, ministry does go on. True succession continues in the preaching of the gospel. People are baptized, married, and buried. These sermons provide some modest examples.

20

Engaged in the Ministry

2 Corinthians 4:1-7:

> Therefore, since it is by God's mercy that we are engaged in this ministry, we do not lose heart. We have renounced the shameful things that one hides; we refuse to practice cunning or to falsify God's word; but by the open statement of the truth we commend ourselves to the conscience of every one in the sight of God. And even if our gospel is veiled, it is veiled to those who are perishing. In their case the god of this world has blinded the minds of the unbelievers, to keep them from seeing the light of the gospel of the glory of Christ, who is the image of God. For we do not proclaim ourselves; we proclaim Jesus Christ as Lord and ourselves as your slaves for Jesus' sake. For it is the God who said, 'Let light shine out of darkness,' who has shone in our hearts to give the light of the knowledge of the glory of God in the face of Jesus Christ. But we have this treasure in clay jars, so that it may be made clear that this extraordinary power belongs to God and does not come from us.

Crisis in the Ministry

Churches today have become greatly perplexed about the ministry. Some years ago Peter Berger, a well-known sociologist of religion, wrote a letter to his nephew, who was thinking about going into the parish ministry as his life's vocation. He responded to charges heard at the time that the parish ministry was in suburban captivity—irrelevant, ineffective, morally ambiguous, and generally absurd. H. Richard Niebuhr wrote in his famous study, *The Purpose of the Church and Its Ministry*: "The contemporary church is confused about the nature of the ministry. Neither ministers nor the schools that nurture them are guided today by a clear-cut, generally accepted concept of the ministry." Joseph Sittler wrote his famous *Christian Century* article, "The Mascerated Ministry," bewailing the fuzzy image of the ministry. Decades of ecumenical dialogues on the ministry and numerous task forces appointed to study the ministry have provided no solutions to the problems of identity-crisis, burn-out, drop-out, or negative feedback. Vice President Spiro Agnew coined the funny phrase, "nattering nabobs of negativity." It applies to much of the contemporary analysis. A lot of negative talk and a dark cloud of uncertainty have enveloped the ministry.

What a contrast to the apostle Paul! He said, "Having this ministry, by the mercy of God, we do not lose heart." How could Paul be so sure? He had no guarantees, no union card, no pension plan, no master of divinity degree, no ordination certificate, and no license to preach. How could he be so positive that he knew what the ministry was all about? Paul had reason to reconsider his calling. He recounted his experience:

> Many imprisonments, countless beatings, often near death. Five times he received the forty slashes save one, three times beaten with rods, once stoned, three times shipwrecked, nights and days adrift at sea, in danger from rivers, danger from robbers, danger from his own people, danger from the Gentiles, many sleepless nights, hungry and thirsty.

In addition Paul bore the pressure of carrying the burdens of the churches in Corinth, Rome, Ephesus, Thessalonica, and even Jerusalem. He had every reason to be stressed out.

Why are we moderns so negative? Why was Paul so positive? We have all the modern approaches that provide surgical analysis of all our problems. We have exegetical studies, historical and confessional studies, sociological and psychological expertise, and at the end of the day, we have more questions than when we began, suffering from a paralysis of self-analysis. What is our problem? What was Paul's great secret? It was not the power of positive thinking. It was not some "how-to-do-it" manual. It was not some bag of tricks.

The Ministry Is God's, Not Ours

Paul was imbued with three convictions that raised his strong sense of ministerial identity to the highest possible pitch. The first is that his ministry was not his own; it belonged to the one who sent him. It was God's own ministry; it came to him the day he met Christ. It was not his own scheme, not something he chose to do simply because his daddy told him he would be pretty good at it, nor was it because he was tired of making tents and looking for an easy second career. The ministry was not a profession that would bring dignity, honor, status, special prerogatives, privileges, and perquisites. It was by the call of God that Paul knew who he was and what he was to do. It was a grace-event that gave him a vigorous sense of his own importance and an intense conviction of having been ordained to be a hand-picked instrument in the hands of God.

There can be no substitute for that. No synodical committee, no faculty review process, and no career lab results can take the place of this unique and indispensable appointment to ministry from the Spirit of God who works quietly in the inner recesses of one's soul. If that sense is missing, none of us would last long in the ministry. It would not even take beatings, imprisonments, or torture by third degree. None of us is strong enough to remain in the ministry on our own strength and perseverance. Paul cried out, "Who is weak, and I am not weak? . . . If I must boast, I will boast of the things that show my weakness" (2 Corinthians 11:29a-30).

The Content of the Ministry

The second secret to Paul's confidence was that he knew the content of his ministry. He knew what he was to preach or, better, whom he was to proclaim. He could use different words for the content of his preaching. At times he called it the word of God or the light of the gospel. But clearly Paul did not preach himself. Nor did he preach the latest fad or fashion in theology. He did not preach any ism. He did not tell cute stories to tickle the ears of his audience. He did not learn his theology from one of the prestigious synagogues in Jerusalem.

I came upon a book written by a person touted as being among the most avant-garde in theology. This author wrote: "Paul, Aquinas, Luther, and Tillich all assumed that faith refers to something real, an experience of ultimacy that is in some way actual and present, an ultimacy that limits and shapes the nature of theological inquiry." Then this pseudo-authority wrote unabashedly: "We modern academic theologians no longer have the surety of such a referent." Presumably we sophisticated moderns cannot be sure about what is real and true. We cannot be sure that God is real, that God cares. or that God has spoken his final word in Jesus Christ. In fact, that is like confessing that we modern academic theologians don't know what we are talking about. We have no message, of course not, when we insist on trying to get the message out of ourselves, to dig it out of our own minds, hearts, and experience. It is like trying to drill for water in the Sahara desert.

Not so with the apostle Paul. His message was clear, coherent, and centered in Christ. Paul had seen the light of the gospel of the glory of Christ, who is the very image of God incarnate. Paul said, "For we do not proclaim ourselves; we proclaim Jesus Christ as Lord" (2 Corinthians 4:5).

The problem with our studies of the ministry is that we analyze ourselves; we tally up the pressures and take the soundings of our culture, and then ask: Where does the ministry fit in? What jobs does the minister need to perform? We start at the wrong end and wind up in a state of confusion. We worry about the minister's status, authority, job description, compensation, and retirement benefits—all things that have some small degree of importance. But altogether they do not amount to anything of lasting consequence if the transcendent message is not clear. The message is the gospel, the light of the knowledge of the glory of God in the face of Christ. That is so simple that any child can believe it. And it is so profound that no theology can exhaust its mystery.

Servants in the Ministry

The third aspect of Paul's secret for a strong sense of pastoral identity is this: Always remember who is the master and who is the servant. We are earthen vessels, not the good stuff inside. We are the servants, Paul said, for Jesus' sake. It is a salutary thought to know that in the kingdom of God, service is not a stepping-stone to something higher. It is the end in itself; service is our only product, not a means to an end.

Luther said, "The true treasure of the church is the holy gospel of the glory and grace of God. This treasure, however, is understandably the most hated thing, because it makes the last to be first, and the first to be last." That is the definition of a revolution.

It is important for us to keep these things ever in our minds. No doubt, members of the call committee and members of the congregation which we are called to serve are looking for skills in relating to people, skills in administering the parish programs, and skills in leading public worship, leaning not too much this way and not too much that way. They want their pastor to be a good preacher, perhaps not a prophet; strong on evangelism and stewardship, perhaps not a Bible teacher; a sensitive and caring counsellor, perhaps not an advocate for social justice. Studies show that people want their pastors to have a personality with a degree of charisma—positive, open, flexible, and able to manage conflict while remaining cool under pressure. They want their minister to exhibit piety and a life morally beyond reproach.

All of these expectations add up virtually to an impossible task, amounting to a no-win situation. No one, not even Paul or John or Peter, could possess all the charismatic gifts which the Spirit distributed to members of the one body of Christ. They did not need them. Moreover, they did not need all the skills, credentials, talents, and personal charm that, of course, we would all like to have our pastors possess.

Paul knew that God does not necessarily choose servants from the cream of the crop:

> Consider your own call, brothers and sisters; not many of you were wise by human standards, not many were powerful, not many were of noble birth. But God chose what is foolish in the world to shame the wise; God chose what is weak in the world to shame the strong; God chose what is low and despised in the world, things that are not, so that no one might boast in the presence of God (1 Corinthians 1:27-29).

It is a humbling thought, but also liberating, to know that we are called as pastors to be servants, not to show how smart we are, not to climb to the top of the ladders of power, prestige, and popularity, not to become superstars in the galaxy of the church hierarchy or paragons of moral virtue. We are called to be faithful servants willing to sacrifice everything for Christ and his people. This is a subject about which it is difficult to speak in our time, in an affluent church that does not call for much sacrifice, but prefers to reward success in terms of worldly standards. It seems rather too much for any of us to claim that, as ministers of the Word, we have devoted ourselves to a calling that requires total sacrifice, total self-surrender to Christ and self-giving to our people. But precisely that describes Paul's strong self-identity as a minister of Jesus Christ and his church. This truth conflicts with the fact that if we meet our people's expectations, even halfway, we will hardly be broken and poured out in soul, even unto death. It conflicts with the fact that the ministry compares favorably with many other occupations, if not always in material rewards, at least possibly in terms of ego-gratification and public status. Those who today are preaching the gospel of prosperity and wealth are the false prophets leading people astray with their deceits in the name of the Lord.

Paul warns, "Do not tamper with the Word of God." Let your approach be nothing but the open statement of the truth in the sight of God and every person's conscience. These strong words are clues to the secret of Paul's doctrine of the ministry. Paul would not sell the gospel at a cut price. We have this same ministry today. It is only when we practice the ministry at a reduced price and water it down to be just another job that we can do on our own, that we get all the problems about which the professional analysts like to remind us.

We are wise not to let the clouds of negativity envelop our ministry today. Nothing has happened in our century or any other century since the first one that makes Paul's great secret to a faithful ministry in Jesus' name less real and relevant for us than it was for him. Amen!

21

Believing and Behaving as Disciples

Luke 9:51-62:

> When the days drew near for him to be taken up, he set his face to go to Jerusalem. And he sent messengers ahead of him. On their way they entered a village of the Samaritans to make ready for him; but they did not receive him, because his face was set toward Jerusalem. When his disciples James and John saw it, they said, "Lord, do you want us to command fire to come down from heaven and consume them?" But he turned and rebuked them. Then they went on to another village.
>
> As they were going along the road, someone said to him, "I will follow you wherever you go." And Jesus said to him, "Foxes have holes, and birds of the air have nests; but the Son of Man has nowhere to lay his head." To another he said, "Follow me." But he said, "Lord, first let me go and bury my father." But Jesus said to him, "Let the dead bury their own dead; but as for you, go and proclaim the kingdom of God." Another said, "I will follow you, Lord; but let me first say farewell to those at my home." Jesus said to him, "No one who puts a hand to the plow and looks back is fit for the kingdom of God."

Jesus' Call to Discipleship

Jesus set his face to go to Jerusalem. He was on his way to the cross. He had chosen a path that would lead to great suffering and a horrible death. For several years Jesus had been preaching the gospel of God's coming kingdom: "Repent and change your lives and believe in the gospel." He confronted people with a clear "either/or." Choose either God or mammon, either the way of the spirit or the way of the flesh. Either go with the flow of the worldly majority or swim against the stream with the faithful minority.

But Jesus did not want to go it alone. He called some to go with him—the disciples. He chose Peter and his brother Andrew, a couple of fishermen, and said to them, "Follow me," and they left their nets and followed him. He called a man named Matthew, a tax collector, and said, "Follow me," and Matthew left his collection booth and followed Jesus.

Thus, Jesus built up a band of disciples who walked along with him, preaching from village to village, healing the sick, casting out demons, and teaching the way of God's kingdom. There were many who wanted to tag along. They wanted to be a part of this new movement. Exciting things were happening, never a dull day. Wherever Jesus went, he attracted a crowd. People wanted to get close to him, to hear his voice, touch his clothes, and see him do something awesome, like making a blind man see or a lame man walk.

Then Jesus set his face to go to Jerusalem, and once again, as he was walking along the road, he renewed the challenge, "Follow me." Three people stepped forward and said, "Yes, I will follow you wherever you go." But then they began to lay down their conditions. Yes, I will follow you, Jesus, but first I must take care of business. Yes, I will follow you, Jesus, but first I must go back home and talk it over with the folks. Yes, I will follow you, Jesus, but not until I have had some time for myself. When I get older, then I'll join the movement and get on the road with Jesus that leads to Jerusalem.

When Jesus said, "Follow me," he never promised it would be cheap and easy. He said to his disciples, "If any want to become my followers, let them deny themselves and take up their cross and follow me" (Matthew 16:24).

Dietrich Bonhoeffer, a German Lutheran pastor, answered the call to follow Jesus, and it led him into a Nazi prison cell. Then on April 9, 1945, five days before the Allies liberated the prison camp, he met his death at the hands of the S.S. Black Guards.

Bonhoeffer wrote a now famous book with the title, *The Cost of Discipleship*. It is a scathing criticism of what he called "cheap grace." "Cheap grace," he said, "is the deadly enemy of our church." Cheap grace is cutting the cost of what it means to follow Jesus. "Cheap grace," he said, "means the justification of sin without the justification of the sinner." Cheap grace is grace without price, grace without cost! Cheap grace means that you can become a Christian and nothing needs to change. Everything remains the same—the same old ideas and the same old lifestyle. The world around us goes on its merry old way, and meanwhile we Christians live our lives not remarkably different from the rest of the world.

Cheap grace, Bonhoeffer said, is offering forgiveness without repentance, baptism without church discipline, and communion without confession. Cheap grace is grace without discipleship, saying we believe in God, yes, but without the will to follow Jesus. The Gallup poll says that ninety-five percent of us Americans believe in God, but like the three would-be disciples on the road to Jerusalem, we also have our private reasons and excuses not to follow Jesus.

There is no guarantee that the first step in baptism will necessarily result in a life of faithful discipleship. Discipleship calls for discipline, training, education, and sacrifice. That is where we come in as sponsors and parents, even as an entire congregation. We are making promises on behalf of an infant, regularly to bring her to church, teach her the Bible and the catechism, and show by personal example how to live a God-pleasing life.

Cheapening the Cost

Since the time of Emperor Constantine in the fourth century, the church has practiced infant baptism. A few churches protest this practice and do not baptize infants, their reason being that it makes grace cheap. The church is dispensing the sacraments of grace at cut prices. In Western European countries almost everybody gets baptized. Almost everybody is counted as Christian. In England less than five percent of the people attend church on Sunday; in Norway and Sweden the figure is about the same. Teeming millions of baptized people are growing up to believe and behave like pagans in the so-called Christian nations of the West. About them David Hart has said they've been "lightly baptized." Cheap grace is giving people the illusion that they can be Christian without following Jesus, the deception that baptism without discipleship, without following it up with a disciplined Christian life, is acceptable church practice.

What does it mean to follow Jesus? Earnest believers have asked that question in every age. The answer does not remain the same for everyone, everywhere, and always. St. Francis of Assisi heard the call of Jesus, "Follow me," along with the instruction to "go and repair my house [the church], which is in total disrepair." At first Francis interpreted this command in a literal sense. He started repairing church buildings that were in bad shape. Gradually it dawned on him that he was to repair not this or that building but the very church of Christ on earth. He followed Jesus into a life of poverty and attracted many others to join the Order of Friars.

But not all disciples have done it the way of St. Francis. History has preserved for us a letter written by an early Christian writer which said:

> Christians are not distinguished from the rest of humanity either in locality or in speech or in customs. For they do not dwell off somewhere in cities of their own, neither do they use some different language, nor do they practice an extraordinary style of life. . . . They dwell in their own countries but only as sojourners. . . . Every foreign country is a fatherland to them, and every fatherland is a foreign country (*The Letter to Diognetus*).

This means you cannot tell followers of Jesus by the way they dress, the hats they wear, what they eat, or the language they speak. There are Christians, of course, who have tried to distinguish themselves as disciples of Christ by their external appearance and peculiar lifestyle. Martin Luther held such a notion as a young man. On a hot day in July in 1505, Luther was walking from one town to another, when suddenly the sky became overcast. It began to rain, and then a bolt of lightning knocked him to the ground. He saw his life passing before his eyes, and he cried out, "St. Anne, help me! I will become a monk." As a student of Scripture Luther learned later that Jesus' radical call to follow him does not necessarily mean that one must become a monk or seek a vocation inside the walls of the church.

Ordinary Disciples

Followers of Jesus tend to be quite ordinary folks, pursuing faithful lives in their daily vocations. They are following Jesus in their own way in the grubby world of power politics, community building, family life, and earning a living. They are quite ordinary saints who follow Jesus in their work as policemen, nurses, farmers, executives, teachers, factory workers, not shirking the moil and toil of their daily routines. We cannot follow Jesus onto a "religious reservation" out there in some romantic never-never-land. In our situation the road to Jerusalem with Jesus passes through the world of everyday life, with all its problems, decisions, hopes, and disappointments.

So what is the difference? Perhaps you have heard the story about the three masons building a cathedral. When asked what they were doing, the first mason answered, "I am building a wall." The second said, "I am working so that I can purchase food and clothing for myself and my family." But the third mason said, "I am building a house of God so that people may come and worship and be joyful." All three were doing the same thing, but one found a meaning that the others did not.

Perhaps you would like to follow Jesus wherever he will lead you. Perhaps you have thought about it, and you realize that the cost is high and that you cannot delay payment by using a credit card. Perhaps you realize that it is a matter of life or death. "For those who want to save their life will lose it, and those who lose their life for my sake, and for the sake of the gospel will save it. For what will it profit them if they gain the whole world but forfeit their life?" (Mark 8:35-36).

Perhaps you would like to follow Jesus, but there is just that one thing holding you back, like these characters in our text. "First let me go and bury my father." "First let me say goodbye to the folks at home." You have your reason; I have mine. Perhaps you would like to follow Jesus, but all your secret desires and passions are getting in the way. You do not want to let that old self die in exchange for a new one. But that is exactly what the call of Jesus in baptism entails.

Reaffirming Baptism

Luther taught that the good news of baptism is that "the old Adam in us, together will all sins and evil lusts, should be drowned by daily sorrow and repentance and be put to death, and that the new man should come forth daily and rise up, cleansed and righteous, to live forever in God's presence" (Small Catechism, "The Sacrament of Holy Baptism"). St. Paul wrote, "Therefore we have been buried with him by baptism into death, just as Christ was raised from the dead by the glory of the Father, so we too might walk in newness of life" (Romans 6:4).

To follow Jesus today is to reaffirm the promises you made when you were baptized. If you have lost your way, you can find it again by returning daily to your baptism and reclaiming the covenant of God's grace that was sealed with the blood of Jesus and his cross that awaited him on that gory Friday in Jerusalem.

Happy are those who have been saved by grace to accept the cost of discipleship with joy and abandon. Happy are those who have learned the secret that a disciplined life is worth living. Happy are those who discover that the life of faith passes through obedience to the call of Jesus: "Follow me and I will take you on a fishing trip unlike any you have ever known." Amen!

22

Love Never Ends

1 Corinthians 13:4-8a, 13:13:

> Love is patient; love is kind; love is not envious or boastful or arrogant or rude. It does not insist on its own way; it is not irritable or resentful; it does not rejoice in wrong doing, but rejoices in the truth. It bears all things, believes all things, hopes all things, endures all things. Love never ends. . . .
>
> And now faith, hope, and love abide, these three; and the greatest of these is love.

What kind of love is it that never ends? Where can you find it, especially these days when even the most ordinary civic virtues are in short supply? We have all shared to some degree the miracle power of love. Today we are witnesses of the invisible power of love to grasp two different persons, draw them to each other, and set them on the same path, on their way to building a common life.

The love that the apostle Paul writes about is an exceptional love. It is something more than a person can feel; it is much more than romantic feeling, otherwise Paul could not state so daringly that love never ends. Romantic feelings may come to an end, but real love never ends. We see all around us how people come together for a few, fickle, and fugitive erotic relationships, but like our used bottles and machines, we are quick to throw them away.

Paul says, love never ends; it lasts forever. He is not talking about ordinary earthly love. He is talking about divine love, the eternal love of God in which we may participate through faith and hope.

Romantic love is strong enough to bring a man and a woman together, and even to the altar; but faith and hope are needed to mold it into a love that never ends. Paul speaks in the first letter to the Corinthians of the great triad of faith, hope, and love, but the greatest of these is love. Faith will come to an end, when we shall see God face to face. Hope will come to an end, when we reach the goal of fulfillment. But the greatest of these is love, because love will never end. For love is the stuff of life, the eternal secret mystery of life, coming from deep in the heart of God. St. John says: "God is love." That is the best definition of God we know.

Yet love, as necessary as it is, is not sufficient by itself. No matter how great the love between two persons, it needs to be supported by the helping hands of faith and hope. Perhaps we could say that love, all by itself, is blind; so it needs the eyes of faith and the light of hope to channel it and keep it moving forward.

This is where the church comes into play. We do not need the church to get married, but we do need the ministry of the church—the preaching of the Word, the sacraments, and the communion of saints—to keep the fires of faith and hope alive. Theologians debate whether marriage is a sacrament of the church and, if so, in what sense. There clearly is something sacramental about marriage, otherwise it would be pointless to solemnize it in church, invoking the presence and blessing of the Spirit of God.

The church is in the business of preaching the love of God that never ends. This kind of love is best exemplified in the close relation between Christ and his church, between the head and the body, and between all the members of the body of Christ.

In marriage we make a promise for life. A promise is a covenant, much more profound than a legal contract. The promises, the vows, are basic in the mystical union between a man and a woman, husband and wife. The whole Christian life is made of promises. You made promises in your baptism, in confirmation, and now you will make another promise that is valid for life. We can break promises, but we can never nullify them.

Marriage is a great mystery. Two persons become one flesh. It is a kind of sacred arithmetic: One plus one equals one. So we dare to make a promise that opens into a future of life together, even though we cannot know what the future has in store for us. For one thing, we promise fidelity. As God was faithful to his church, so we too promise to be faithful to each other, until death do us part.

The quality of faithful love is sacrifice. Love will never last long without willingness to sacrifice. Love does not insist on its own way; it cares about others for their own sake. As Christ sacrificed himself for our sakes, so also in a marriage mounted on love, each spouse sacrifices for the other in being patient. The word "patience" comes from the Latin word for "suffering." There is pain in such suffering, because it means death to one's own egoism, self-centeredness, and self-indulging arrogance. Only through sacrificial self-control from both sides can there be mutual joy and happiness.

All of this love and mystery and meaning will be symbolized by the exchange of rings. The ring is a token of love, faithfulness, and the will to sacrifice for mutual flourishing and fulfillment.

Under these conditions we can take Paul at his word, that love never ends. Love does not fail under these special conditions of faith and trust in the power of the Spirit to help us keep our promises. Otherwise we would have to settle for romantic love that soon withers and fades away under the heat of anger, jealousy, selfishness, and all the negative passions we are capable of inflicting on each other.

So let us give thanks as a Christian community that God has promised to add his blessing to this marriage, that as you give yourselves to each other, you are not on your own. God will be with you through thick and thin, good times and bad times, because God's love is not fickle and feeble. God will see you through to the end of the journey, because he promises to be with us always, until the end of our time. So on the basis of God's promise, we can rejoice to hear Paul's good word for today: Love shall never end! Amen!

23

O Death, Where Is Your Victory?

1 Corinthians 15:54-57:

> When this perishable body puts on imperishability, and this mortal body puts on immortality, then the saying that is written will be fulfilled:
> "Death has been swallowed up in victory.
> Where, O death, is your victory?
> Where, O death, is your sting?"
>
> The sting of death is sin, and the power of sin is the law. But thanks be to God, who gives us the victory through our Lord Jesus Christ.

The words of the apostle Paul are as fresh as when he wrote them. Many things have changed since the time of the early Christians, but one thing has not changed—the universal sting of death and the unique promise of victory through the resurrection of our Lord Jesus Christ.

Death is still a mystery to us. No matter how much we are benumbed by the scientific temper of mind, with our knowledge of biology, psychology, and neurology, death is still a mystery. The fact that death is the destiny of all life is completely baffling. Life is a being-unto-death, said the philosopher, Martin Heidegger. St. Paul would agree with that. Death is also a lonely event. St. Augustine said, it is the only thing that is absolutely certain and inescapable. Everyone will die, and die just once. Before we die we do lots of dying; it is a process that is continually going on within us. But death itself is fatal and final.

All around us we see that death is bearing down upon us. We have become a death-oriented people, whose economic engines are working overtime to produce ghastly instruments designed only to kill. Killing in our society has become big business. We are all into it very deeply, every last one of us.

What choices do we have in face of the inevitable and universal fate of dying and death? Our world offers two responses: The one is to laugh it off; the other is to sink into despair. One is frivolous, and the other very earnest. Is that not why so many people indulge in loud and noisy entertainment to drown out the voice that comes from the grave? "Keep awake therefore, for you do not know on what day your Lord is coming" (Matthew 24:42). "For we will all stand before the judgment seat of God" (Romans 14:10). "It is appointed for mortals to die once, and after that the judgment" (Hebrews 9:27).

One of the kings of France commanded that the subject of death never be mentioned in his presence, for somehow it had a way of upsetting him. We moderns have learned nothing that gives us any advantage over the ancients when it comes to coping with our mortality and perishability. We have become masters at covering it up.

The other response to death, other than laughing it off, is to sink into despair. This too is widespread, anxiety being the disease of our age. There are serious people collapsing in despair, without hope for a future of life beyond the grave. There is no rainbow sign on the horizon of life. Everything is dark and gloomy—no hope of sharing in the eternal glory of Christ, only fear; no confidence in the meaning of life, only confusion; no over-arching trust in the providence of God, only blind mechanisms at work in nature and history.

When Christianity entered the stage of world history, death was pictured as a tyrant that keeps people enslaved by fear, filled with anxiety about the unknown future. That is when Paul wrote these defiant words: "Where, O death, where is your victory? Where, O death, is your sting?" (1Corinthians 15:55). Something new entered into the world of our human experience and history, to change our outlook on the future and our attitude toward death. All Christians united with Christ through baptism in the congregation of the faithful now rejoice in the hope of sharing in the eternal glory of God far beyond the reach of death.

We believe in our hearts that Christ came to do battle against death and gained victory through his resurrection from the dead. That is what Easter is all about. Every Christian funeral service is an Easter event, a suitable occasion for Handel's "Hallelujah Chorus." Never for a moment do we believe that death is the last word; it is the beginning of a new phase of life. The perishable puts on the imperishable; this mortal nature puts on immortality, Paul says in the same letter.

As much as we are scared to death of dying according to our natural state of mind—and who would deny that that is the case?—on account of Christ's victorious resurrection, death has lost its terrifying power. The sting of death has been pulled; the grave can no longer claim victory. It is the threshold leading to a new state of fulfillment.

During an epidemic in the ancient church, Christians observed that they were dying right along with their pagan neighbors. The angel of death played no favorites. Then Cyprian, the bishop of Carthage and great church father from North Africa, wrote a letter to his church members saying:

> You must not mourn for those who are released from the world by the call of the Lord, when you know that they are not lost, but sent on before, that they may go ahead of those who are left behind, as travelers or voyagers. We must indeed long after them, but not bewail them. We ought not, for their sakes, to put on black garments, since they are already clothed in white. We must not give unbelievers an opportunity to blame Christians for sorrowing for their loved ones whom they speak of as living with God, as if they were lost souls and had perished, and thus denying the truth of what they confess outwardly in words by the witness of their hearts.

Many wonder why this life simply should not be enough. Why ask for more? Why do we creatures of time long for eternity? The poet has written, "Hope springs eternal in the human breast." Even if we lived as long as Methuselah, it would not be long enough, because our hearts are restless, longing for a fulfillment this life will not grant. It belongs to our nature to hope for a fulfillment beyond time, beyond the borders of this earthly existence. We long for the peace of God, the eternal *shalom*, that we can only partly experience in this life. We long for total freedom beyond our craven attachment to worldly things. We long for perpetual light that will not be overtaken by darkness. We long for a love that will outlast our selfishness. We long for complete perfection purged of all sin and evil. That is why we believe that in heaven we will have crossed the threshold of time into the everlasting communion of life in the Triune God, Father, Son, and Holy Spirit. By raising Jesus from the grave, God has put the deadly power of death to death. The power of his resurrected life begins to work already here and now in the church, the body of Christ, in the power of the Spirit, through the forgiveness of sins, by the preaching of the Word and the celebration of the sacraments.

Our Christian belief in the victory of God through our Lord Jesus Christ allows us to celebrate the life of our departed loved ones, who will enjoy in a way we can all only anticipate, the glory of a fulfilled life, that transcends in boundless measure the imperfections and limitations of our earthly existence.

All that is good in this life, God will raise up and establish in the glory of his perfection. All the love and the beauty and the selfless service to others that our loved ones have shown will be raised up to the highest power in the kingdom of God, as they join the company of the blessed saints who have kept God's word, who have remained loyal to the Lord, and loved the church they so faithfully served to the end. Amen!

PART SIX

Death and Resurrection

Eschatology is a word that comes from the Greek meaning "last" and "study." In Christian theology eschatology deals with the "last things," the final events in the history of the world and of humankind. Since they deal with what has not yet happened, hope and not knowledge is the appropriate category to relate to the future. Hope lies at the heart of human existence. Where there is life there is hope, and where there is hope there is religion. The religion that best responds to the universal human quest for a total hope founded on truth is what we claim for Christianity. Christian hope is not a guessing game; it does not indulge in wishful thinking. Christian hope is based on the resurrection of Jesus of Nazareth. In this event God brought everlasting life out of the finality of death. If Jesus would not have been raised from the dead, the cause of God's kingdom for which he lived would have died with him. There would have been no church and no one to remember Jesus' words and deeds.

The power of resurrection hope rests on two conditions—that it really happened to Jesus and that it means what the New Testament says it means. We have no theory to explain the miracle of the resurrection, but that is no reason to doubt or deny it.

Some modern Protestant theologians, for example, leaders of the "Jesus Seminar," are of the opinion that Christian faith is possible apart from belief in Jesus' resurrection in particular and life beyond bodily death in general. These sermons affirm, to the contrary, that the resurrection of Jesus defines who God is. God is the one who raised Jesus from the dead and on that account promises everlasting life to those who believe.

24

God Put Death to Death in Raising Jesus

1 Corinthians 15:25-26:
> For he must reign until he has put all his enemies under his feet. The last enemy to be destroyed is death.

In the Eastern Orthodox Church it is customary on Easter to greet a friend with the words, "Christ is risen!" and as you shake hands, the other person responds, "He is risen, indeed." I have noticed that this wonderful tradition is now widely practiced in other churches. It underscores the fact that apart from belief in the resurrection, the Jesus movement would have died along with all the other first century Palestinian liberation movements. Christianity would never have entered the mainstream of world history.

John Masefield wrote a passion play in which one of the characters tells Pilate's wife of Christ's death. The governor's wife asks, "Do you think he's dead?" When the answer is given, "No lady, I don't," she asks, "Then where is he?" And the man replies, "He's let loose upon the world, where no one can stop him."

The resurrection of Jesus gave impetus to the Christian faith. The conviction of the women—Mary Magdalene, Joanna, and Mary, the mother of James—was that Jesus is risen. He is alive and no one has been able to stop the Easter parade of witnesses to the power of the living God in a doomed and dying world.

As a student of history, do you remember the dates of all the battles, the coronations of emperors, and the rise and fall of nations? List the ten most important events in the history of the world, and you will see that not a single one has exerted a more profound influence on the lives of people than the resurrection of Jesus of Nazareth from the grave.

The Empire of Death

Jesus entered into a vast empire of death, with its network of rulers, authorities, and powers. They all conspired to put Jesus on the cross and into the grave. He was "crucified, died, and was buried." God was willing to go to extreme lengths to enter fully into the fate and destiny of our human life and world.

We do live in a world of decadence and death. From Plato in ancient times to Martin Heidegger in modern times, death has been called the "muse of philosophy." There is nothing like death to concentrate the mind and drive a person to ask about the ultimate meaning of life. The existentialist authors—Sartre, Camus, and others—explored every variation on the theme of our existential subjection to the universal law of death. But they never spoke of resurrection. Looking deeply into the abyss of death, they dramatized the dark side of experience into which our Lord entered through his suffering and death. What did they tell us? They told stories about how everything becomes unbearable, ridiculous, and hopeless because all of life is swallowed up by death, with no trace of joy or any ultimate meaning and purpose. They were bearing out what Paul wrote, "If for this life only we have hoped in Christ, we are of all people most to be pitied" (1 Corinthians 15:19). If Christ has not been raised from the dead, everything we are and do falls into the abyss of nothingness.

Simone de Beauvoir, one of the French existentialists almost as famous as her husband, Jean-Paul Sartre, wrote about the death of her mother in her book, *A Very Easy Death*. The daughter cared for her mother during the progressive stages of dying. She told about how death shook her own confidence in life and how she became totally revolted. She could not talk to her mother about her inevitable death. She had to go on kidding her mother that her illness could be cured and that she would soon get better. She did not know what to say to comfort her mother. She lived only in the awareness that death involves sinking into absolute nothingness, with no hope, light, victory, or Easter, to tell a different story.

Paul says it so well, without faith in the victory of Christ, we are certainly no match for the most powerful enemy in the world. "The last enemy to be destroyed is death" (1 Corinthians 15:26). The existentialists tell us so eloquently what life looks like under the mesmerizing spell of death.

When I was a young man, just out of college, existentialism was all the rage, something like deconstructionism today. I went newly married to Paris to study the French existentialists. There for one year I nourished my mind on their dreadful philosophy and stories, about hopelessness, monotony, boredom, chaos, absurdity, emptiness, madness, futility, loneliness, not to mention anxiety, guilt, despair, and nausea, until I got sick of it. All they could tell me was to have courage, to accept my fate, and to grope around in the dark alleys of life haunted by death. There welled up within me a deep hunger and thirst for life, for an eternal power of being mightier than death.

On Good Friday Jesus went into this kind of death and went all the way to hell. He learned first hand the universal fate and unavoidable destiny of every human being. It was a horrible death; he died the death of a sinner. It was not a glorious hero's death. Jesus died in bitter despair, feeling lost and even separated from his Father. He experienced everything the existentialists were driving home to us. He did not give us tidbits of wisdom about courage and resolve. He gave us victory on Easter morning, three days after he died such a death. That brings new life, new zest for living, a boundless hope, and a new dynamism. Instead of Sartre's definition of hell as being "other people," Jesus went to hell to liberate the captives. He gave us a profound concern for people and a new capacity to love in a world that is choking on hate.

But not everyone is as honest as these existentialists. Ernest Becker has written a great book entitled, *The Denial of Death*. If we cannot face death in the light of Easter's victory and enjoy the radiant hope of the resurrection, we might try to indulge ourselves in the denial of death.

There are people today who apply all their science and technology to outwit death by the use of refrigeration techniques, dreaming of a future in which death will be totally abolished. Then science will succeed in thawing out the frozen bodies and bringing them back to life to live forever. In less far-fetched ways people are busy trying to cover up their fear of dying, through their toys, drugs, the pursuit of pleasure, and the acquisition of power. We cover death with flowers, perfumed cosmetics, and sentimental music, trying to put a pretty face on our ugly and bitter enemy. Some pretend that death does not scare them at all. They live by the ancient dictum: "Eat, drink, and be merry, for tomorrow we die." Rousseau called the bluff of these people when he said, "Those who say that they're not afraid of death are a bunch of liars." If death is no big deal, there is no point in talking about the resurrection. If death is not the last enemy, then Easter is not the last hope. All we have to get excited about are eggs, lilies, and bunnies.

Putting Death to Death

Death is a super-power. It is stronger than any of the other super-powers, authorities, and rulers of this world. William James called death "the worm at the core" of our existence; it eats away at the meaning of life. There is really nothing we can do about it. But there is also within each of us a deep hunger for lasting life, for eternal life, to rise beyond death into the everlasting circle of God's infinite life and boundless love, wherein God will be all in all, and mean absolutely everything to everyone. Most religions reflect a longing for a life that will not be destroyed by death. But there is not a thing we can do to produce such a life out of our dying world. That is why Easter is so special. Christ is risen; he is alive. That is the message the earliest Christians believed and proclaimed.

Jesus did not come to bring a new philosophy better than that of the Greeks. Jesus did not come to bring a new law better than that of Moses. Jesus did not come to bring a new mystery religion better than that of the Persians. Jesus did not come to bring a new political system better than that of the Romans. Jesus came to bring us a victory over the last enemy of life and humanity—death and its deadly poisons. The whole empire of death, with all its rulers, authorities, and powers have been put under his feet; he has destroyed the sovereignty of death. He has stomped on its head and put it to death. Jesus said, "I came that they may have life, and have it abundantly" (John 10:10). That is true because he has broken the back of this last enemy. This enemy has been put to death. Jesus' battered body that was laid away in the grave as a corpse has been raised a spiritual body alive in the world today. Because of that, not death but Christ has the last word.

Well, you might ask, what difference does it make? Tell us about it! Don't we all still have to die? Don't we all still have to face our death, even on this side of Easter? So, where's the victory? Where's the good news? What's all the celebration and cheering about? Why are we singing all these "Hallelujahs"? Are we one whit better off than the existentialists say we are?

If it is true that God has raised Jesus from the dead, there are dramatic consequences. It tells us, first of all, what kind of a God we have; he is a God of power. If he is able to break the bondage of death, he is a powerful God. The power that God used to create the world out of nothing he now uses to create a new world out of death. God is the power of the new creation; he creates a new world in which death will rule no more.

If Jesus is raised from the dead, that tells us that God is a God of justice. If Jesus had given his whole life to bring in the kingdom of God, having remained faithful and perfectly obedient to his mission, even unto death, and if God would have let him lie in his grave forever, he would not be a God of justice. If the living God, powerful enough to create life, would let death swallow up the life of Jesus and all the love he had poured out to sinners, to sick and dying people, and that were all there were to it, we could not believe in a God like that. Nor could we believe in a God of love, because by leaving Jesus in the grave, God would have shown that love is no match for hate, that love is weak and useless. It would give the last word to crime, murder, brutality, and all the dirty things that were done to God's own beloved Son.

But if God has raised Jesus from the dead, he has thereby demonstrated for us his true nature, that ours is a God of power, justice, and love, all in the face of the last enemy of humankind.

Christ is risen, and he is alive as our leader in the struggle against death in our bodies, families, businesses, and society. In our baptism we were recruited to wage war against all the works and ways of death. In our baptism we were united with Christ in his death and resurrection. In Holy Communion we do not remember a leader who fell in battle, who is now dead and gone. We do not meet in a graveyard. We do not gather around his tombstone. In breaking the bread and sharing the cup, we commune with the living Lord who is risen and alive in our fellowship.

The struggle against death is not over. It continues in our life. In one of his Easter sermons Martin Luther said: "Just as Christ won the victory only through struggle, so also must we. If his resurrection is to work in us, we too cannot escape the struggle with death. . . . This is the fight, and we must say, 'Death, I will be thy death.'"

That is the meaning of our gathering together every week on the Lord's Day. Our day of worship was changed from Saturday to Sunday, because Easter is the first day of the new creation. We celebrate that day each week as we come to church. People sometimes ask, "Why do we need to do that every week? What's so important about going to church?"

A man was driving through Kentucky one Sunday, and he came upon a field in which there were several hundred mules. He was curious to know why so many mules were gathered in one place, so he stopped to ask the man in charge. "What are all those mules doing here?" The man answered, "The mules work in the coal mines. We bring them up one day a week into the sunlight, or they would go blind."

Without gathering around our leader in the struggle against death in our world, in the sunlight of Easter, we would become morally and spiritually blind. We would drift along with the ways of the world that lead to death, decay, and decadence.

Through the Word and the sacraments in our gathered fellowship, the power of the resurrection is released into our hearts, and we use that power in our struggles against death, at home and at work. The deadliness of death is rampant in our society. There is a deadness in our relationships, in the breakdown of our family life. There is a deadness in many marriages. There is a deadness in our work. As Studs Terkel pointed out in his study on work, the percentage of people who enjoy their work and find meaning in it is very small. There is death in our sexual life, which is a God-given gift to bring life and fulfillment: instead, it spells death, disease, and moral collapse for many millions of people. Marilyn Monroe was the sex symbol *par excellence* for a whole generation. She seemed to have everything—success, lovers, publicity, beauty, and wealth. But in August 1962 she took an overdose of sleeping pills to end it all. It was a Saturday night, and she was lonely. She had lost her will to live. Death came to Elvis Presley and many other icons of success, including Michel Jackson, the king of pop music. Ernest Hemingway committed suicide, and Dylan Thomas died in despair.

There is a deadening of values and of morality in political life—as witness the numerous indictments and trials of persons in high public office. There is death in drugs—LSD, heroin, cocaine, crack. Death is a refrain in many of the lyrics of rap music.

Life Beyond Death

We could go on and on, pointing to more traces of death and destruction in our contemporary scene. The point is not to paint an overly pessimistic picture, to make us appear more dead than alive. The point is to remind us as believers that Easter is not only a celebration of Christ's victory but also an invitation to join the struggles against all life-destroying activities in our world.

When our life's struggle is over and we come to the end, the Easter victory gives us the assurance that "neither death, nor life, nor angels, nor things present, nor things to come, nor powers, nor height, nor depth, nor anything else in all creation, will be able to separate us from the love of God in Christ Jesus our Lord" (Romans 8:38-39). We need this assurance as we journey to our own death, that finally "if we live, we live to the Lord, and if we die, we die to the Lord; so then, whether we live or whether we die, we are the Lord's" (Romans 14:8).

Dietrich Bonhoffer was engaged in a life and death struggle against Hitler's deadly system. On the last day of his life in prison, Bonhoeffer held a little service for his fellow prisoners on Sunday, April 8, 1945. One of the men who lived to tell about it said:

> It seemed that God was real and close to him. He spoke to us in a manner which reached the hearts of all, finding just the right words to express the spirit of our imprisonment. He had hardly finished his last prayer when the door opened and two evil-looking men in civilian clothes came in and said, "Prisoner Bonhoeffer, get ready to come with us." Those words "come with us"—for all prisoners they had come to mean one thing only—the scaffold.
>
> We bade him goodbye—he drew me aside—"This is the end. But for me the beginning of life."

Bonhoeffer's secret confidence lay in the power of the resurrection, God's Easter victory. It opened the door that had been locked since death entered the world through the sin of Adam and Eve.

Thanks be to God who gives us the promise of victory through the death and resurrection of our Lord Jesus Christ. Amen.

25

Lazarus and Jesus: Thoughts on Death and Resurrection

John 11:1-6:

> Now a certain man was ill, Lazarus of Bethany, the village of Mary and her sister Martha. Mary was the one who anointed the Lord with perfume and wiped his feet with her hair; her brother Lazarus was ill. So the sisters sent a message to Jesus, "Lord, he whom you love is ill." But when Jesus heard it, he said, "This illness does not lead to death; rather it is for God's glory, so that the Son of God may be glorified through it." Accordingly, though Jesus loved Martha and her sister and Lazarus, after having heard that Lazarus was ill, he stayed two days longer in the place where he was.

When I was a child attending a parochial school, our teachers had us learn and recite Bible passages by heart, some times whole chapters and lengthy Psalms. Memorization was a must. On special occasions we were supposed to choose a passage to recite out loud in group devotions. One of the most frequently chosen Bible verses—inevitably someone would choose it—was from the Gospel of John. It is the shortest verse in the Bible. The slowest among us could remember it. It simply says, "Jesus wept." Jesus cried because one of his best friends had died. Lazarus was dead, and now Jesus' favorite family in Bethany was in mourning. Mary and Martha had lost their only brother, and Jesus was deeply moved and troubled. He assured Martha that her brother will rise again. Martha thought he meant that he would rise at the end of time. Then Jesus spoke the whole gospel in a nutshell: "I am the resurrection and the life. Those who believe in me, even though they die, will live, and everyone who lives and believes in me will never die" (John 11:25). You will hear these familiar words at almost every Christian funeral. Then Jesus went to the tomb where Lazarus had been for four days. They rolled away the stone, and Jesus cried out with a voice loud enough to wake the dead, "Lazarus, come out." Many of the Jews who saw what he had done believed in him. But others went to tell the chief priests and Pharisees, and from that time on they plotted to kill Jesus.

We are in the season of the church year that moves us toward the celebration of the death of Jesus on the cross and his resurrection from the grave. But even now, on this side of Good Friday and Easter, the church is asking us to listen to its message about death and resurrection, and to do so in a way that does not steal the thunder of Easter. Let us say, we are doing our warming up exercises before getting into the full swing of Holy Week and Easter.

The Other Side of Death

Lazarus had not fallen into a deep sleep. He had died. He had been in the tomb for four days, and decay had begun to set in. Then he was raised from the dead. But this was not a real resurrection. Lazarus was only returning to the life he had known before; he would have to experience dying all over again. A real resurrection means one has gone through death and out the other side, never to return to the same old mode of existence. What happened to Lazarus was no resurrection; it was a resuscitation, a restoration to life in the same mortal body, warts and all, that went into the grave. But still this was a miracle.

Some people say they do not believe in miracles. We live in an age of science, skepticism, and scoffing. To believe in a miracle is to believe in the power of God to do a wonderful thing, something totally unusual and against the grain of ordinary human expectation. This miracle was performed, not for its own razzle-dazzle quality, not to make spectacular drama, but "it is for God's glory, so that the Son of God may be glorified through it" (John 11:4b). Jesus raised Lazarus from the dead to magnify and glorify God, and to make the point that his resurrection soon to come would be of another dimension. Jesus did this so that people might believe that he is "the resurrection and the life." Though our death is bound to come, already now through faith we have a share of eternal life through our being in Christ and through the indwelling of his Spirit in us. We have a foretaste of the resurrection already now before the general resurrection at the end of time.

Can we still believe in the miracle of resurrection, still place our hope in the miraculous power of God to see us through death and to the other side? Well, where did belief in the resurrection come from? It began with the Jews, during the time of their exile in Babylon—which was somewhere in Iraq. The Jews in exile struggled daily with the question of their faith, whether God had forgotten them, especially all the faithful ones who died under pagan rule and domination. Had they trusted and believed in God in vain? Would Israel perish forever in enemy territory, with no hope for the future? Then the prophet Ezekiel had a vision of the valley of dry bones. The dry bones will live again; the dry bones will put on flesh and sinews, covered with skin, and begin to breathe and live again. There is hope for Israel after all beyond the exile. There is hope for restoration to the promised land. The God of Israel would restore his people. Those who died in the struggle, loyal to him and his Torah, would be raised from the dead to share in the eventual restoration. The righteous ones who have been killed by their pagan masters are for the present at peace, safe in the arms of God, and at last they will be raised to share in the blessings of the age to come.

Christianity took over this Jewish belief in resurrection. There is no real Christianity without it. Resurrection is the Christian answer to the question, when a person dies, is that all there is to it? Is death the last word? Because God raised Jesus from the dead, death is defeated; death is demoted to next to last, no longer the very last thing. But death is real. Lazarus was really dead. And the death that Jesus was soon to die was also very real.

It is more fun to talk about resurrection than about death. Many more Christians go to church on Easter than on Good Friday. I have a pastor friend in Seattle, Washington, who wrote in his pastoral letter to the congregation, "Don't plan to come on Easter without first coming on Good Friday." Why? Because death and resurrection belong together. Resurrection is God's answer to the universal human question about death. If there is no question, there is no need for an answer. If death is not real, there is no need for a real resurrection. The agony of Good Friday comes first, then comes the ecstasy of Easter.

We live in a death-denying culture. The reason is that people know in their guts that death is real and frightening. The fear of death is universal and profound. What do we do when we do not have an answer to a problem or predicament? We deny it. This is why Americans spend billions covering up the stark reality of death. We paint a pretty face on it. We try to make the dead look as life-like as possible, like the dead are only sleeping. We wish to make death seem a little less harsh, less real, less fatal. So we order a lot of beautiful flowers—too late for the deceased to enjoy. We also speak in polite euphemisms about death, like "passed away," "called home," "fell asleep."

As Christians who believe that Jesus is the resurrection and the life and have pinned their hope on the victory of Jesus over death, we have a different way of dealing with death. First of all, we do not deny it. Like everyone else, we have a natural fear of death. We know that death is inevitable. Methuselah lived a long time, but eventually he too had to die. Death is mysterious. We do not know what is on the other side. And death is a lonely experience; each one of us must face it alone. We can not hold hands and all jump in together. Like everyone else we Christians also experience grief and sadness, because it hurts to be separated from the ones we love. Because death is so real and frightening, some religions deny it. They talk about immortality, transmigration, or metempsychosis, as though death is only a station on a long journey that never ends.

To the contrary, the Bible is very realistic about death. Death is no friend of ours. It is an alien with catastrophic power to annihilate life. It is truly an enemy of life. So it is understandable that people should fear and resist death.

As baptized and believing Christians we are equipped with a secret weapon against this deadly enemy. We have been given by grace a sure and lively hope in the power of God, that just as he was able to create the world out of nothing, God is able to create new life out of death. This hope is a well-founded conviction that in Jesus' resurrection God put death to death. God replaced the deadliness of death with the joyful knowledge that not even death can separate us from the love of God. So also there will be no eternal separation form the ones we have known and loved in our earthly experience.

The Difference Hope Makes

When I was a parish pastor I observed that people behaved very differently at funerals. Families that had lapsed from the faith, never went to church and had forsaken Christian practices, would be completely shattered by the death of a family member. They had to face death with no hope, no assurance of eternal life. They seemed scared to death of death. They feared the worst; perhaps hell was real after all. Who knows? In sharp contrast Christian families, faithful church members, people who knew in whom they believed, though grieving and sad at the loss of a loved one, were still able to encounter death with peace in their hearts, in the blessed assurance that because of Jesus' resurrection, death is a conquered enemy.

I witnessed the same contrast in Madagascar, where my father and mother were missionaries. When a heathen person died, village life would come to a stand-still. The natives would be paralyzed, tormented by the fear of evil spirits on the loose, some of them the angry spirits of unhappy ancestors. The witch doctors would then go to work to appease the spirits by offering sacrifices of cattle, sheep, or goats. The relatives of the deceased would flail about in loud grief-stricken wailings, sometimes continuing for days.

What a beautiful contrast to see how faith in the resurrected Christ, the faith the missionaries brought, conspicuously impacted and transformed the behavior of the Malagasy people. The Malagasy Christians could now hope for life beyond death, for eternal life on the other side. Death has been put to death. The sting of death has been pulled. Gloom and despair have given way to peace and joy. They could now sing, "Glory, glory, hallelujah!" What a contrast, obvious to anyone with eyes to see.

We live in a religiously pluralistic world. Especially after 9/11 people are becoming more interested in other religions, their beliefs and practices. Naturally the question arises, aren't all religions basically the same? Is Christianity unique? What is the difference? The difference is this: While all religions have their founders, gurus, and prophets, with commanding personalities, only Jesus has been raised from the dead, to be the Lord and Savior of the world. Only Jesus has a name that is above every name, so that at the name of Jesus every knee shall bow, and every tongue confess that Jesus Christ is Lord, to the glory of God the Father. Only Jesus is the resurrection and the life, not Buddha, Mohammed, Lao-tzu, Joseph Smith, or Mary Baker Eddy. Apart from his resurrection Jesus would have been only a prophet, not the Messiah, and Christianity would be just one among many world religions, with no gospel to tell to the nations.

Perhaps we wonder sometimes whether it pays to be a Christian. What's the benefit? Are we more successful? Any better off? Are we healthier or happier? More popular, more safe and secure? I am not sure about all that, but I am sure that because we believe in Jesus as our risen Lord, we anticipate our death differently, and because we die differently, we live with the sure hope that death will not extinguish the flame of life forever. Though we die, we shall live again and be reunited with all those saints who have gone before. We will not come back to life like a Lazarus. We do not hope for that. But we do hope that because of Jesus, who is the resurrection and the life, we will go into death and out the other side, to be with all the saints and the angels in the company of heaven forever and ever. God's victory over death gives us hope not only for ourselves, but also for a new world in the kingdom of God, a world where there will be no more violence, kidnappings, holocausts, terrorism, nuclear weapons, disease, weeping, and no more dying. That is a lot to hope for, but to hope for anything less would be to diminish the scope of the power and the glory of God's victory over death in the resurrection of Jesus. Amen.

26

The Last Things

Mark 13:21-22; 13:32-33:
> And if anyone says to you at that time, 'Look! Here is the Messiah!' or "Look! There he is!"—do not believe it. False messiahs and false prophets will appear and produce signs and omens, to lead astray, if possible, the elect. . . . But about that day or hour no one knows, neither the angels in heaven, nor the Son, but only the Father. Beware, keep alert; for you do not know when the time will come.

The Apostles' Creed ends with a statement of Christian belief in "the resurrection of the body, and the life everlasting." The second article of the Nicene Creed states that Jesus Christ "will come again in glory to judge the living and the dead, and his kingdom will have no end." Eschatology—from the Greek word *eschata*, meaning "last things"—is the technical word for the Christian vision of the future end and fulfillment of history and the cosmos.

The Present and Future Kingdom

Christianity began as an eschatological faith, but it did not start from scratch. Eschatology was also a constitutive part of the story of salvation in the Old Testament. The prophets announced the day of Yahweh, the coming of the Messiah, and the new Jerusalem, looking forward to a new and different future in history. In the book of Daniel and in the period between the two Testaments, Jewish eschatology became apocalyptic. In apocalyptic writings we find visions of a wholly new future of history, a new age above and beyond this one.

Jesus' message of the kingdom can best be understood within the milieu of late Jewish apocalypticism. In the world of apocalyptic literature we read about Satan, angels, demons, dragons, aeons, signs of the times, the millennium, cosmic catastrophes, resurrection of the dead, the last judgment, the end of history, and the final restitution of all things in God. All these things together add up to what the Christian tradition has called "the last things." Who can understand what they mean?

Jesus said, "Let anyone with ears listen!" (Matthew 11: 15) In the Apocalypse of John we read, "Let anyone who has an ear listen to what the Spirit is saying to the churches" (Revelation 2:7). Apocalypse means revelation, hence the unveiling of hidden mysteries and meanings. It takes something like apocalyptic imagination to grasp "the things which are above" (Colossians 3:1).

There are three unsatisfactory approaches to the "last things": 1) to construct a travelogue or literal timetable of events that will happen in the near or distant future; 2) to interpret the images as metaphorical expressions of religious experiences and inner states of mind unrelated to real history and the future; 3) to reduce apocalyptic literature merely to social commentary or subversive rhetoric of an oppressed community in times of persecution.

Though there may be some truth in these approaches, the great tradition of church teaching has interpreted eschatology by keeping Christ at the center. The central motif of Jesus' message was the kingdom of God. This was a favorite theme of the "social gospel" movement. It symbolized social values and political ideals worthy of human striving. But the "social gospel" reduced eschatology to ethics. In that era, Albert Schweitzer gained theological fame by recovering the full eschatological meaning of Jesus' preaching of the kingdom of God. The kingdom is the power of God breaking in upon the present world, not the crowning fulfillment of its progress. The kingdom comes on God's own terms, not as a result of human cooperation and calculation.

Jesus began his ministry announcing that the day had come for God to begin his reign, that his kingdom was about to be realized in history. For his Jewish audience this could only mean that the eschaton was at hand. The hope of Israel was that when God comes in the power of his rule, the world will really change. The arrival of God's kingdom will bring a turnabout of all things, putting an end to misery, poverty, and even death.

Jesus did not merely announce the coming of a future kingdom, like one of the Jewish prophets. For Jesus the kingdom of God was at once a present reality, functioning in his very person and ministry, and a promise of fulfillment still to come. Then suddenly something surprising happened; Jesus was crushed by the ruling powers of his day. The fulfillment he expected was shattered on the cross. But soon after the crucifixion there arose a core of friends and followers witnessing to the reappearance of the crucified Jesus. This was good news: God had raised Jesus from the grave, a kind of event that Jews expected to happen only at the end of time. Surely, it dawned on them, this must be an eschatological occurrence, the beginning of the end. Henceforth, for Christians resurrection hope will forever be founded on the person of Jesus, the Messiah of God, the bringer of the new age. "Christ the first fruits, then at his coming those who belong to Christ" (1 Corinthians 15:23).

The Mission to Change the World

The paradox for Christians is that if the kingdom has already arrived in Jesus, why do things look pretty much the same A.D. as B.C.? The hope of Israel was that when the Messiah comes, God would at last destroy all resistance to a permanent establishment of peace, justice, and freedom. That would spell an apocalyptic transformation of the world. So why, since the Messiah has come, has the world not changed in a fundamental way?

The answer is that it has; world history has been changed by the missionary proclamation of the church. The good news of the kingdom has been preached throughout the world, the Bible has been translated into every tongue, and churches have been planted among the nations. Somewhat cynically, Alfred Loisy said: "Jesus preached the kingdom of God; but what came was the church." The church was founded at Pentecost as the community of the end-time. The community of believers lives between the times, between the first coming of the Messiah Jesus in the flesh and his final advent in glory at the end of time. The future eschatological kingdom is already present for those who are in Christ. In worship believers sing of a "foretaste of the feast to come."

The Revelation of John identifies Christ as the one "who is and who was and who is to come" (Revelation 1:4; 1:8). It is noteworthy that the present tense comes first. The risen Christ is really present in the community of believers according to the Spirit. However, the risen Christ is none other than Jesus of Nazareth whose story the gospels tell. And the crucified Jesus who is the risen Christ will come again in glory to judge the world. Christ is the Alpha and the Omega, the beginning and end of all things, the Lord of history and the cosmos.

The "last things" are not like a runaway train that takes off on its own. Everything must be tethered to Christ. He is the basis of resurrection hope. His is the promise of eternal life. All things will be subject to his judgment in the end. There is no way to the Father's heart except through the Son. All the so-called "last things" cohere in Christ. Faith generates hope that in the end the power that God displayed in raising Jesus from the dead will transform the world and triumph over the forces of sin, death, and the devil.

Meanwhile, before the "last things" come to pass, Christ is present in his church by virtue of his Spirit. Under his authority the renewal of the world is under way through the missionary witness of his people. But a struggle is going on between divine and anti-divine forces. Even though their days are numbered, Satan and his servants are on the loose, making martyrs of those who witness to the victory of Christ. That is why the church lives in anticipation of the parousia of its Lord, who cries out: "Surely I am coming soon." And the church responds in its eucharistic prayer, "Amen. Come, Lord Jesus!" (Revelation 22:20).

For many today the images of biblical hope seem to have lost their magnetic pull. The sense of transcendence remains strong enough perhaps to say "no" to the way things are, but too weak to construct a positive scenario of the future. In modern existentialism only a sense of crisis prevails; nothing but nothingness looms in the future. Marx does offer a revolutionary model of utopian hope—the oppressive system can be changed—but this ideology too has failed. Theologians have looked to biblical eschatology for a hopeful alternative. In doing so they have also worried about whether or how it is still possible and relevant to believe in the eschatology of the Bible.

Can we who live in a secular age governed by a scientific mindset still share the hope of the first believers, using their language and idioms? All sorts of interpretive schemes have been used to purge the Bible of its supposedly naive images of the future. We cannot go into them here, but they have one thing in common—all references to the future are converted to the present. And that is a mistake. The parousia, the end of the world, the final judgement, the second coming of Christ, the resurrection of the dead, and everlasting life—all these are understood not as pointing to real events or a real future. Instead they supposedly serve merely as signals of transcendence, symbols of existential experience or goads to ethical seriousness.

There is a better way. The time dimension of the future not only belongs to biblical eschatology, but is also deeply rooted in the structure of each human being. Not only are hopes the genes of biblical faith, but hope is essential to meaningful existence. There is a profound connection between biblical eschatology and the phenomenon of hope. It is our belief that what the Bible conveys is true concerning the history of promise, resurrection hope, the future of Christ, and the consummation of the world. Amen!

www.ingramcontent.com/pod-product-compliance
Lightning Source LLC
Chambersburg PA
CBHW050320120526
44592CB00014B/1985

RELIGION | PREACHING

Pluralism as such is not the enemy of the gospel.

Preaching the Christian message will always encounter a world with many religions, world views, ideologies, and lifestyles. The earliest generation of Christians found themselves in a pluralistic situation. They were witnessing to Jews as well as to Greeks and Romans in the great melting pot of Hellenistic culture.

Religious pluralism does pose a threat when it becomes an ideological dogma that asserts that all religions are equally valid and lead to the same goal. Many of the sermons in this volume challenge the pluralistic theology of religion that effectively nullifies the Great Commission to preach the gospel to all the nations.

These sermons are mostly didactic; they teach the faith. They are doctrinal; they assert and defend the truths of the classical Christian tradition. These sermons are unabashedly Christocentric in that they enter into the most controversial issues of Christology today. In the long run the only thing that will sustain the church is firm confidence in the biblical truth that God revealed himself in the life, death, and resurrection of Jesus.

Bratten says:

> The church is utterly different from the world; the gospel it proclaims is unique to Christianity and different from other religions and ideologies. The church through the generations proclaims there is salvation in no other name than the holy name of Jesus the Christ. That is not in accord with the popular pluralistic theory of religions, but that is where we wish to take our stand, no matter how much that might offend what is deemed to be politically correct.

The Rev. Dr. Carl E. Braaten is a graduate of St. Olaf College, Northfield, Minnesota; of Luther Seminary, St. Paul, Minnesota. He has studied at Heidelberg University, Oxford University, and has advanced degrees from Harvard Divinity School. He has served as a parish pastor, an instructor at Luther Seminary, and for thirty years as professor of systematic theology at the Lutheran School of Theology at Chicago. He was a founder of the Center for Catholic and Evangelical Theology and served as its executive director from 1991 to 2006.

Along My Garden Path

Poems on the Rhythms of Life

Holly W Schwartztol

with illustrations by
Vincent Ostertag